Summary of Contents

D0775305

JUMP START SASS

BY HUGO GIRAUDEL
& MIRIAM SUZANNE

Jump Start Sass

by Hugo Giraudel and Miriam Suzanne

Product Manager: Simon Mackie   **English Editor**: Kelly Steele
Tech Editor: Kaelig Deloumeau-Prigent   **Cover Designer**: Alex Walker

Published by SitePoint Pty. Ltd.

48 Cambridge Street Collingwood
VIC Australia 3066
Web: www.sitepoint.com
Email: business@sitepoint.com

ISBN 978-0-9941826-7-8 (print)

ISBN 978-0-9943470-1-5 (ebook)
Printed and bound in the United States of America

About Hugo Giraudel

Hugo is a French front-end developer and writer working at Edenspiekermann in Berlin, Germany. Since discovering Sass in 2012, he has devoted a lot of time assisting the Sass community, as well as authoring SassGuidelines, SassDoc, and hundreds of articles on front-end technologies. In his spare time Hugo likes to work on open-source software, hang out with his cats, eat French cheese, and play pool—not necessarily in that order. You can find him on Twitter at: https://twitter.com/HugoGiraudel.

About Miriam Suzanne

Miriam Suzanne is an author, performer, musician, designer, and web developer. She has been an active member of the Sass community since developing the Susy layout toolkit in 2009. Miriam creates web software with OddBird, music with Teacup Gorilla, novels and poetry with [WriteyWrite], theater with Vicious Trap, and Lego spaceships with anyone who is interested. She is also the author of Riding SideSaddle* (a multimedia open-source novel), and The Post-Obsolete Book (a performable website).

About SitePoint

SitePoint specializes in publishing fun, practical, and easy-to-understand content for web professionals. Visit http://www.sitepoint.com/ to access our blogs, books, newsletters, articles, and community forums. You'll find a stack of information on JavaScript, PHP, Ruby, mobile development, design, and more.

Table of Contents

Foreword

When I started contributing to the features and development of Sass more than eight years ago, I'd never have predicted that one day it would reshape the face of modern front-end web development. But these days, Sass is a staple technology for web developers and designers. It may not be right for every project, but you absolutely must have Sass in your toolbox.

Even more exciting to me is the amazing community of smart, talented, and enthusiastic designers and developers that has sprung up around a technology created to help front-end developers build stylesheets in a more reusable and maintainable way. From meetups to dedicated conferences, people around the globe have come together to share their excitement for Sass—clearly there's more going on here than in your standard web development tool!

Over the years, two of those community members, Miriam Suzanne and Hugo Giraudel, have become some of the most notable users and creators of Sass plugins and best practices for how to use Sass effectively. Miriam created one of the most well-known grid system frameworks, Susy[1], along with a wonderful testing tool named true[2], for ensuring that Sass code is working correctly. Hugo's writing on websites such as Sass Guidelines[3] has set the standard for how to wield Sass effectively, while his plugins have pushed Sass to the very limits of what's possible. Both have left an indelible mark on Sass, both in the community and on the technology itself. Moreover, they are trusted advisors when early feedback is sought on new features that are being added to the language.

If you're yet to learn Sass, there's no time like the present. I suggest that you jump start your learning of Sass right now with this book. The combined expertise of these authors with more than a decade of learning and crafting world-class websites using Sass means that you're in great hands.

Chris Eppstein, Sass Core Developer

---

[1] http://susy.oddbird.net/
[2] http://oddbird.net/true/
[3] http://sass-guidelin.es/

Who Should Read This Book

This book assumes reasonable familiarity with HTML and CSS. You don't need to be familiar with JavaScript or any programming language, although some experience would be helpful. No prior experience with Sass or any other CSS preprocessor is assumed.

Conventions Used

You'll notice that we've used certain typographic and layout styles throughout the book to signify different types of information. Look out for the following items:

Code Samples

Code in this book will be displayed using a fixed-width font, like so:

```
<h1>A Perfect Summer's Day</h1>
<p>It was a lovely day for a walk in the park. The birds
were singing and the kids were all back at school.</p>
```

If additional code is to be inserted into an existing example, the new code will be displayed in bold:

```
function animate() {
  new_variable = "Hello";
}
```

Where existing code is required for context, rather than repeat all the code, a vertical ellipsis will be displayed:

```
function animate() {
  ⋮
  return new_variable;
}
```

Some lines of code are intended to be entered on one line, but we've had to wrap them because of page constraints. A ➡ indicates a line break that exists for formatting purposes only, and should be ignored:

```
URL.open("http://www.sitepoint.com/blogs/2015/05/28/user-style-she
➥ets-come-of-age/");
```

Tips, Notes, and Warnings

Hey, You!

Tips will give you helpful little pointers.

Ahem, Excuse Me …

Notes are useful asides that are related—but not critical—to the topic at hand.
Think of them as extra tidbits of information.

Make Sure You Always …

… pay attention to these important points.

Watch Out!

Warnings will highlight any gotchas that are likely to trip you up along the way.

Supplementary Materials

https://www.sitepoint.com/premium/books/jssass1

The book's website, containing links, updates, resources, and more.

http://community.sitepoint.com/

SitePoint's forums, for help on any tricky web problems.

books@sitepoint.com

Our email address, should you need to contact us for support, to report a problem, or for any other reason.

Want to take your learning further?

Thanks for choosing to buy a SitePoint book. Would you like to continue learning? You can now gain unlimited access to ALL SitePoint books and courses plus high-quality books from our selected partners at SitePoint Premium[4]. Enroll now and start learning today!

---

[4] https://www.sitepoint.com/premium/home

Chapter 1

Hello World!

Welcome, fellow developer! I heard you wanted to learn about Sass. How adventurous! Worry not, my friend, as we will be your guides during this incredible journey, walking you through ten chapters in no time so that you can start using Sass in your day-to-day projects.

From learning about variables and mixins, to how to structure your project architecture—this book will cover the basics of the language in a detailed, informative, and fun way.

CSS in Modern Front-end Development

The creation and maintenance of our projects on the Web has advanced as the Web has progressed. Where we were once perhaps webmasters, the many, varied disciplines involved in making websites and applications has diversified. Front-end development is now one of many roles required in making today's websites. A front-end developer will generally now produce HTML, CSS, and JavaScript for a web application or site so that its visitors can access the content and interact with it.

With modern websites providing more content in various ways and with most web makers adopting an approach that incorporates responsive web design principles, we're now writing more complex CSS than ever before. Add to that how CSS is an ever-changing language, with more and more features added to its existing set every year.

CSS practices and methodologies such as OOCSS[1], SMACSS[2], ITCSS[3], and BEM[4] (to name but four) are excellent tools and processes that help with writing stylesheets and keeping us sane in this modern era of front-end development. Yet, creating CSS for a responsive, device-agnostic website using OOCSS and BEM can lead to thousands of lines of code in one cumbersome file.

We will soon explore how Sass can help you with this. But if you happen to be a total beginner on the matter, you might even be wondering …

What is Sass?

Sass is a stylesheet language that is *an extension of CSS*. It is one of a few preprocessors (more on that in a bit) available to the front-end developer. As it has been around the longest (of the aforementioned preprocessors), we could agree with the official website[5] when it reports to be the "most mature, stable, and powerful professional-grade CSS extension language in the world."

Using Sass helps eliminate some of the monotony and overhead from writing CSS. No longer will you have to remember that specific hex color code for the company's brand. Say goodbye to one long CSS stylesheet or additional HTTP requests, as well as increased page load times by splitting up your CSS files to several files such as **reset.css, mobile.css, tablet.css, desktop.css** and **print.css**. Want an easier way to write CSS media queries? Sass has you covered. Like using ems or rems but hate working out the math? Sass can help you.

All in all, we can safely state that Sass will make it easier for you to develop websites and web applications—benefiting you, your client, and your clients' users. Keep

---

[1] http://oocss.org/
[2] https://smacss.com/
[3] http://itcss.io/
[4] https://en.bem.info/
[5] http://sass-lang.com

your work in check and minimize opportunities for broken designs using the power of Sass.

Sass may have its downfalls but, generally, problems that developers find with Sass are usually when they struggle to understand some aspect of it. With this book, we hope to give you the building blocks to write awesome Sass code. But you will require a firm grasp of CSS as well; if you write bad CSS in the first place, you'll end up writing bad Sass too. You might be familiar with the saying "Tools do not output bad code. Bad developers do." Remember, Sass is just a preprocessing tool, which leads us to our next section.

What is preprocessing?

As mentioned, Sass is a **preprocessor**. It takes Sass (**.sass**) or SCSS (**.scss**) files as input, and outputs CSS files (`.css`). Sass adds a lot of great features that can help to create better stylesheets, but as you know, web browsers only understand CSS, not Sass. What we do is write our CSS (with as much a sprinkling of Sass as needed) in **.scss** or **.sass** files in our code editor, and then have Sass compile that into a `.css` file for the browser to read.

Using a preprocessing language such as Sass means we're not bound within the limitations of CSS. Sass can—and does—add features that enhance our writing of CSS; however, it does not—and cannot—add features to CSS itself. It's vital that you grasp this from the outset.

The Tale of Two Syntaxes

When talking about Sass, we usually refer to the preprocessor and the language as a whole; for example, a Sass project, or a Sass variable. Meanwhile, Sass (the preprocessor) allows two syntaxes:

1. Sass, also known as the *indented syntax*
2. SCSS, or *Sassy CSS*, a CSS-like syntax

Let's pause for a moment for a short history lesson. Initially, Sass was part of another preprocessor (that still exists) called Haml[6], which was heavily inspired by the

---

[6] http://haml.info/

programming language Ruby. Sass stylesheets used a Ruby-like syntax with no braces or semicolons, and a strict indentation:

```
.media
  margin: 10px
  overflow: hidden

.media .img
  float: left
  margin-right: 10px
  display: block

.media .content
  float: right
  margin-left: 10px
```

This was up until 2009, when the new `.scss` file format was introduced that adhered more closely to the usual CSS syntax. The rule of thumb here is if it is valid CSS, it's valid SCSS:

```
.media {
  margin: 10px;
  overflow: hidden;
}

.media .img {
  float: left;
  margin-right: 10px;
  display: block;
}

.media .content {
  float: right;
  margin-left: 10px;
}
```

As to which syntax to use, the choice is really up to the author as both are strictly equivalent in features. The Sass indented syntax is shorter and lighter to type because almost all punctuation is gone, but it's also incompatible with default CSS syntax.

It would appear that SCSS is the most popular in the Sass community as it is closer to CSS and has an easier learning curve, contrary to the whitespace-sensitive syntax of Sass. Because of this, we'll be using SCSS in the code displayed throughout this book.

Note that "Sass" is never uppercase, no matter whether we're talking about the language or the syntax. Meanwhile, "SCSS" is always uppercase. You could use http://SassnotSASS.com/ as a reminder.

 SassScript

You might have heard of SassScript, the actual scripting language used by Sass. The Sass interpreter then translates SassScript into CSS. This is not vital information, just a something to be aware of.

LibSass

There are two primary implementations of the Sass compiler: one in Ruby, and another (called LibSass) in C/C++. People often wonder which one is official, or better. The short answer is that you can use either one; they are both official. The latest versions should be fully interoperable with each other, and new features will be released in tandem from here on.

The long answer starts in 2007 with a different language called Haml[7], mentioned in the previous section. Hampton Catlin[8] designed his HTML Abstraction Markup Language to provide a more structured and easier-to-read templating language for HTML. Before long he had added Sass to the project, bringing a similar look and feel to CSS. For several years Haml and Sass were packaged together in the Haml Ruby gem. At that point, many users saw Sass as a *syntax* improvement on CSS, with very few additional features.

Eventually, people started to realize that Sass had more to offer than a whitespace-aware syntax. Nesting and variables grew into mixins, functions, loops, and conditions (features we'll discuss in upcoming chapters). Sass grew bigger than Haml, and split off into its own project with Natalie Weizenbaum[9] at the helm. Still, it remained a Ruby gem, and was most popular with teams that already used Ruby in their projects. Others were weary of adding such a large new language dependency.

---

[7] http://haml.info/
[8] https://twitter.com/hcatlin
[9] https://twitter.com/nex3

As Sass grew and third-party Sass tools became more powerful, compilation times began to drag. The combination of speed and portability issues gave Hampton a new idea. In 2013, at the first ever Sass Conference, he announced the arrival of LibSass: a C/C++ port of the Sass engine. Developers started flocking to LibSass, speculating that it might be the end of Ruby Sass, even though it was far from compatible with it at the time.

It wasn't the end, but it did divide the community between two versions of the language for some time. That's why a year later at SassConf 2014, Chris Eppstein[10] and Weizenbaum announced a feature-freeze on Ruby Sass, enabling LibSass a chance to catch up. The plan was to align both engines with an external specification, and then develop and release future features together.

So far, it's gone exactly according to plan. A major development push on LibSass was led by Marcel Greter[11] and Michael Mifsud[12], where feature parity (or something close to it) was announced at SassConf 2015. LibSass now has wrappers available for Go, Java, JavaScript, Lua, .Net, Node (with Gulp and Grunt plugins), Perl, PHP, Python, Scala, and even Ruby. The two engines are fully compatible, and Sass is back in development mode. Sass 4 is underway with exciting new features.

There is still work to be done documenting the Sass specification and writing tests for any Sass implementation against which to develop. LibSass now has all the official Sass features working to the best of its knowledge, but without shared tests, parity will never be certain. In the meantime, I've tried to document the features available in different versions of Ruby Sass and LibSass with the Sass Compatibility[13] project.

Alternative Processing Tools

As with most aspects of the web industry, there are always alternatives. Although it was first to market, Sass now shares the land of CSS processing with other open-source projects. Stylus, Less, and PostCSS also assist with writing CSS, just like Sass.

---

[10] https://twitter.com/chriseppstein
[11] https://github.com/mgreter
[12] https://twitter.com/xzyfer
[13] http://sass-compatibility.github.io/

Each tool has a different approach, but ends up being quite similar to the other options when it comes to features.

Stylus[14] is built in Node.js. If Sass tries to stay conservative in regard to the CSS language, Stylus is usually more permissive, implementing a lot of features that you'd consider "too much for CSS". Additionally, Stylus is very flexible with the syntax: you can safely omit most bits of punctuation without risking a compilation error.

Less[15] is fundamentally different to Sass, despite looking similar in a number of ways: it is a declarative language while Sass is imperative. The difference, while subtle, implies a few things. When it comes to explaining the difference between Less and Sass, Matthew Dean explains it best[16]:

> A **declarative language** (my emphasis) describes to a machine what we want, and an **imperative language** tells the machine how to do it.
>
> ...
>
> What that means is that Less extends the CSS language under the same declarative model, whereas Sass is a programming language whose syntax is based on CSS. Another way of saying it: both Less and Sass look like CSS, but Sass does not *act* like CSS.
>
> — Less, the world's most misunderstood CSS pre-processor[17]

To be frank, this is quite a deep topic of which very few developers are aware. This is for good reason, as it is of little consequence to know this kind of distinction when authoring stylesheets. All in all, Sass and Less are very similar.

Last but not least, PostCSS[18], which is written in JavaScript, has a different approach as it does nothing more in itself than read your stylesheet. To actually create something out of this tool, you have to configure plugins. A **plugin** is basically an

---

[14] http://stylus-lang.com/

[15] http://lesscss.org/

[16] http://getcrunch.co/2015/10/08/less-the-worlds-most-misunderstood-css-pre-processor/

[17] http://getcrunch.co/2015/10/08/less-the-worlds-most-misunderstood-css-pre-processor/

[18] https://github.com/postcss/postcss

instruction for PostCSS to translate one thing into another. PostCSS enjoys an eco-system of hundreds of plugins; some of them are particularly popular, such as Autoprefixer[19], a plugin that adds vendor prefixes to your CSS based on a given configuration of browsers and versions to support.

But enough talking about the other kids on the block. I assume you chose Sass. And as you'll soon discover, that is a fine choice.

---

[19] https://github.com/postcss/autoprefixer

Getting Started

In the previous chapter, we talked a lot about what Sass actually is and how it can help us bridge the gap between what CSS can offer and what we actually need in our daily routine as web designers. Now is well past the time to start.

As discussed previously, Sass (mostly) exists as both a Ruby gem (sometimes called **Ruby Sass**) and a wrapped C/C++ library (also known as **LibSass**). Additionally, there are a lot of applications for front-end development that take care of everything for you, such as CodeKit[1] or Prepros[2].

We'll now see how to set it up in these environments, starting with the Ruby version.

Ruby Sass

The programming language Ruby handles dependencies as gems. A **gem** is a package that contains program (or script) information along with files to install. Therefore, the sass gem is a package containing everything needed to compile Sass stylesheets to CSS.

---

[1] http://incident57.com/codekit/
[2] https://prepros.io/

To install the Sass gem, you will need Ruby first.

Installing Ruby

On Mac OS, Ruby comes preinstalled so there's nothing further to do.

On Debian or Ubuntu Linux distributions, you need to install Ruby manually like so:

```
sudo apt-get install ruby-full
```

For other less common Linux distributions, I recommend you check the Ruby official documentation[3] to see how to install it properly.

On a Windows machine, you'll have to go through the Ruby Installer[4] setup, a simple program that helps install and run Ruby. It's slightly less straightforward than other operating systems, but what can you do?

Installing Sass

Once Ruby is correctly set up, you can start installing gems, in particular the one we care about: sass. To install it, open a terminal window (on Mac OS, it would be the *Terminal* application, while on Windows, it would be *Ruby prompt*). Then type the following command:

```
gem install sass
```

And that's it! Sass is now installed on your machine and you can use the sass command to compile your stylesheets. You have to admit it was very simple, wasn't it?

 Permission Errors

> If you have a permission error on Mac or Linux, you might need to prefix your command with sudo.

---

[3] https://www.ruby-lang.org/
[4] http://rubyinstaller.org/

Using Sass

Now that you've installed the Sass gem, let's try to use it.

The Sass gem provides a **sass** command that accepts a lot of options. For the sake of simplicity, we won't be covering them all, although we'll still address how to use the basics. See the official documentation[5] for more advanced usages.

In its simplest form, the **sass** command accepts an input file and an output file, like so:

```
sass input.scss output.css
```

When working on stylesheets, it's tedious to execute the former command every time we make a change to the input file. To work around this, we can use what we call a *watcher*. A watcher is a program that detects when a file is being changed, executing a task when it happens.

Sass comes with a built-in watch feature: the `--watch` option. Every time the input file is being modified, Sass will recompile it and override the output file:

```
sass --watch input.scss output.css
```

As we'll discuss in great length in Chapter 9, it is quite uncommon to have just one single Sass file to compile. More often than not, styles are written across a plethora of files gathered in a folder. You will want Sass to compile the whole folder without having to specify a list of files manually. This is how you do it:

```
sass --watch sass/:stylesheet/.
```

LibSass (with node-sass)

As stated in the first chapter, LibSass is unusable on its own and must be wrapped by another library to provide an interface for compiling Sass stylesheets to CSS. The most popular wrapper for LibSass has to be node-sass[6], a Node.js library that compiles Sass to CSS through LibSass.

---

[5] http://sass-lang.com/documentation/file.SASS_REFERENCE.html#using_sass
[6] https://github.com/sass/node-sass

Installing Node.js

To be able to use node-sass, we'll obviously require Node.js. The easiest way to install Node.js is by using one of the installers on the home page of the project[7]. Once done, you'll be able to install node packages, which leads us to the next step.

Installing node–sass

Node-sass is a Node package distributed through npm[8]. It provides both a command-line interface and a JavaScript API to interact with the inner program. Your first task is to install it—either locally in the project with `--save` or globally with `-g`:

```
npm install node-sass -g
```

Using Sass

The command-line interfaces (CLI) of Ruby Sass and node-sass are similar but not entirely compatible so if in doubt, refer to the documentation of the relevant library.

Compiling a single file to CSS is the same as with Ruby Sass:

```
node-sass input.scss output.css
```

You can also add the `--watch` flag in the same fashion to tell Sass to automatically recompile the file on change:

```
node-sass --watch input.scss output.css
```

However, it's slightly different when you want to watch a folder:

---

[7] https://nodejs.org/en/
[8] https://www.npmjs.com/

```
node-sass --watch sass/ --output stylesheets/
```

Wrapping Things Up

All right then. We are now fully ready to actually start writing Sass code. Feel free to create a dummy project on your computer, launch the watcher, and experiment as you progress through the book. There is no better way to learn than by practicing.

Chapter 3

Variables

Variables are at the core of most—if not all—programming languages that ever exis-
ted. A **variable**, broadly speaking, is a storage location paired with an associated
identifier (aka a **variable name**). So a variable is basically made up of a key and a
value, the former being used to retrieve the latter.

When applied to Sass, variables give authors the ability to store bits of content so
that they can be reused throughout the stylesheets. This is especially handy for
colors: one can avoid having countless hues of the same color after a long time spent
working on a project. Variables can also be helpful for storing other types of content
such as font lists, maps of breakpoints, and default asset paths—presumably anything
that you may want to use multiple times across the stylesheet, particularly those
that could be updated at a later point.

A variable in Sass always starts with a dollar sign ($), whether you are using it for
assignment or retrieval. Directly next to the dollar sign comes the variable name,
which is usually made of latin characters, numbers and dashes, or underscores.
Actually, any character can be used as long as it is escaped if needed.

The Same Escape Route

Sass follows the same rules as CSS when it comes to escaping characters in identifiers. For more information about CSS character escape sequences, be sure to
have a look at the eponymous article by Mathias Bynens[1].

For assignment, the variable name and its value are separated with a colon. Finally,
a semicolon ends the statement (in the SCSS version only):

```scss
// Variable assignment
$my-variable: 42px;

// Variable usage
.foo {
  width: $my-variable;
}
```

 Dashes + Underscores = Same

Dashes and underscores are considered the strict equivalent in variable names;
hence, `$my-variable` and `$my_variable` actually refer to the same location.
You could use one to assign the value and the other to retrieve it, and it will work
seamlessly. What's important to remember is that the dash or underscore is a
matter of preference, not syntax.

> [Hyphens and underscores being treated the same] is intentional.
> The rationale is that the separator is a stylistic preference, not
> a meaningful one. — Chris Eppstein, Sass core designer

Data Types

All values in Sass, or rather SassScript (the scripting language itself), are associated
to a specific *data type*. There are seven data types in SassScript:

- `string` (e.g. `"Hello world"`, `kittens`)
- `number` (e.g. `42`, `1337px`)
- `color` (e.g. `hotpink`, `rgb(1, 33, 7)`, `#BADA55`)

---

[1] https://mathiasbynens.be/notes/css-escapes

- `list` (e.g. (a, b, c), a b c)
- `map` (e.g. (a: 1, b: 2))
- `bool` (true or false)
- `null` (null)

Data types are a way for both Sass and those authoring content to know what kind of operations and functions can be run on a specific value. As far as I can tell, all programming languages use some form of typing.

For instance, we can perform mathematical operations with numbers and colors (yes, colors!), but not strings. It is possible to run some specific functions on lists and maps, but not on booleans and null values.

To know the type of a Sass variable, we use the `type-of(..)` built-in function. It returns precisely one of the seven aforementioned types. For more information about how functions work, refer to Chapter 4.

Strings

The `string` data type has to be the most basic type there is since we use it in our life so much, even outside of any computer-related activity. A string is nothing more than a series of characters, such as `Hello world!`:

```
$my-variable: 'Hello world!';
```

In most languages, a string needs to be *quoted*, meaning it should be wrapped with quotes, either double (") or simple ('). In Sass, however, strings do not have to be quoted. It is perfectly fine for a string to live by itself without being wrapped within quotes, as long as non-indentifier characters (latin alphabet, numbers, hyphens, underscores, and spaces) are escaped. Moreover, an unquoted string is—thankfully—strictly equivalent to its quoted counterpart, so that "abc" (or 'abc') is the same as abc. Quoting strings is usually considered best practice, however; not only because it sticks to the syntax of most languages, but because there are some classic gotchas with unquoted strings in Sass when they map with a CSS color keyword (such as red).

String variables are useful for storing some CSS values, property names, or identifiers, such as `sans-serif`, `left`, or `margin-bottom`. When storing string content that maps one-to-one with CSS (such as the three aforementioned examples), we usually omit the quotes because CSS requires them unquoted:

```scss
$font-name: 'Helvetica';
$font-type: sans-serif;

.foo {
  font-family: $helvetica, $font-type;
}
```

Note that it is still possible to quote or unquote a string using the `quote(..)` and `unquote(..)` native functions. For more information about how functions work, refer to Chapter 4.

Strings can be **concatenated** (joined together) using the plus symbol (+). You can thus create a new string from several chunks:

```scss
$base-path: '/images/';
$file-name: 'kittens';
$extension: 'png';
$file-path: $base-path + $file-name + '.' + $extension;
// -> '/images/kittens.png'
```

Numbers

As with strings, numbers are a very basic type of content. I would not dare explain to you what a number is, although I'll point out a very important specificity about Sass numbers before going any further: a number in Sass can—but does not necessarily—have a unit, like 42px.

This behavior, while unconventional at first glance, actually makes sense: you need to be able to perform operations on numbers with a unit just as you run calculations on numbers without. In other words, both 42 and 42px are numbers, while 42 px and px42 are strings.

Returning to CSS, numbers are typically the sort of items you want to store in variables because they're likely to be the moving parts of your application. Think of the maximum width of the container (for example, 1180px), or the number of columns in the grid system in use (such as 12). You want to make those values easily configurable in order to keep the codebase clean and maintainable:

```
$container-max-width: 1180px;

.container {
  width: 100%;
  margin: 0 auto;
  max-width: $container-max-width;
}
```

Obviously, you can perform operations on numerical values. Sass supports the five basic operators: plus (+), minus (-), multiply (*), divide (/), and modulo (%). Some Sass third-party tools such as Compass[2] or SassyMath[3] add extra math features; for example, power (pow(..)), square root (sqrt(..)), Pi (pi()), and so on.

In the following example, we used the $element-width variable as the value for the width property, as well as a way to compute the negative left margin required to horizontally center the element:

```
$element-width: 400px;

/**
 * 1. Size the element
 * 2. Horizontally center the element in its container
 *    @TODO: move to CSS transforms once we drop support for IE 8
 */
.foo {
  width: $element-width; /* 1 */
  position: absolute; /* 2 */
  left: 50%; /* 2 */
  margin-left: ($element-width / -2); /* 2 */
}
```

Before going any further, you might be interested to know that division in Sass is a bit more complex than first expected: the slash symbol (/) actually has a meaning in CSS (think of the font shorthand property). As a result, there are three scenarios in which Sass *does* perform division instead of leaving the / as authored:

- If the value, or any part of it, is stored in a variable or returned by a function.
- If the value is surrounded by parentheses.

---

[2] http://compass-style.org/
[3] https://github.com/at-import/Sassy-math

▨ If the value is used as part of another arithmetic expression.

The following code snippet illustrates these scenarios:

```
.foo {
  $gap: 20px;
  // No variable nor parentheses: no division performed
  font: 16px / 2 sans-serif;
  // Wrapping parentheses: division returning 8px
  padding: (16px / 2);
  // Member as variable: division returning 10px
  margin: $gap / 2;
  // Arithmetic expression: calculation returning 308px
  width: 300px + 16px / 2;
}
```

Units

Before moving on to the next data type, allow me to explain how units are handled in Sass. For starters, units are not just random strings living at the end of numbers; they actually belong to the number. Otherwise, you'd be unable to perform operations on it. That is why the next two examples produce entirely different results:

```
$value: 42;
$good: $value * 1px;
$bad: $value + px;
```

The $good variable multiplies $value with 1px, making the result 42px, a valid number. On the other hand, the $bad variable simply appends the px string at the end of $value, composing a string. While that may seem like small fry, having a string in place of a number is not only inconsistent, it can bring new issues, such as it being impossible to perform any further mathematical operations on it.

As you can guess from the previous example, units in Sass behave the same way in real life. To have 42px from 42, you need to multiply it by one member of the px unit (1px). Similarly, to have 42 from 42px, you have to divide it by one member of the px unit (1px):

```
$initial-value: 42;
$value-in-px: ($initial-value * 1px); // 42px
$unitless-value: ($value-in-px / 1px); // 42
```

For more information about the way units work in Sass, be sure to have a look at this article from me, Understanding Sass Units[4].

Colors

Colors occupy a major position in the CSS language. Sass ends up being a valuable ally when it comes to manipulating colors, mostly by providing a handful of powerful functions, yet there's more it can do.

For starters, a color in Sass—as in CSS— can be expressed in three to four different ways, using:

- the `rgb(..)`/`rgba(..)` CSS functions (for example, `rgb(1, 33, 7)`),
- the `hsl(..)`/`hsla(..)` CSS functions (for example, `hsla(1, 33%, 7%, 0.5)`),
- the hexadecimal notation (for example, `#BADA55`)
- when available, a keyword name (for example, `hotpink`).

 Avoid Color Keywords

CSS color keywords are not recommended, unless for rapid prototyping. Indeed, as English words some of them do a poor job at describing the color they represent, especially for non-native speakers (`chartreuse`, `papayawhip`). In addition, keywords are not perfectly semantic; for instance `gray` is actually darker than `darkgray`, and the confusion between `grey` and `gray` can lead to inconsistent usages of this color.

Any of those notations will make the value a `color`, thus eligible to be manipulated as a color by Sass.

Storing colors is probably the best use case for Sass variables, as maintaining a strict and consistent color chart has proven to be a difficult challenge, especially in large projects. By keeping frequently-used colors in variables, we save ourselves from guessing and inventing new colors:

---

[4] http://www.sitepoint.com/understanding-sass-units/

```scss
$brand-color: #BADA55;

.logo {
  color: $brand-color;
}
```

It improves more so once you start using Sass native color-manipulation functions, such as darken(..), lighten(..), and mix(..). Let's now consider an alert module with different themes depending on the type of message (information, warning, confirm):

```scss
.message {
  padding: 10px;
  border: 1px solid currentcolor;
}

.message-info {
  $color: blue;
  color: $color;
  background-color: lighten($color, 20%);
}

.message-danger {
  $color: red;
  color: $color;
  background-color: lighten($color, 20%);
}

.message-confirm {
  $color: green;
  color: $color;
  background-color: lighten($color, 20%);
}
```

Thanks to the lighten(..) function, it is not only possible but also very easy to create a tint of our color to compute the background color of our message. If you already have an idea on how to optimize this code, hold your horses because we will tackle this in the next chapter!

Booleans

Booleans (or bools, for short) are specific values that exist in almost any programming language. There are only two boolean values: `true` and `false` (written slightly differently depending on the language). Sass sticks to these writing conventions.

Because there is no such thing as a boolean value in CSS, booleans are quite worthless on their own. They become interesting when coupled with conditional statements, introduced in Chapter 5. In the meantime, here's a short example:

```scss
$support-legacy-browsers: true;

@if $support-legacy-browsers {
  .clearfix {
    *zoom: 1;
  }
}

.clearfix:after {
  content: '';
  display: table;
  clear: both;
}
```

As you can see, booleans are perfect to handle toggle-like options, such as *shall we support old browsers?*, *shall we output vendor prefixes?*, *shall we include this module?*, and so on.

The **not** Keyword

Unlike most other languages, Sass lacks a bang operator (`!`) to get the opposite of a value, such as `if (!value)`. Instead, it provides the `not` keyword, which works the same way:

```scss
$bool: false;

// "if not false"
// which can be rewritten as: "if true"
```

```
@if not $bool {
   // We get in there
}
```

 Bang Bang not not

Along the same lines, while being a bad pattern from the C programming world, the very popular "bang bang you're a boolean" technique (!!value) to coerce a value to a boolean is doable in Sass by chaining two not keywords:

```
$value: 'Hello world!';
$coerced-value: not not $value; // true
```

A *falsy* value would return **false**, while a *truthy* value would return **true**. In Sass, only two values are falsy: **false** and **null** (as you will see in the next section), so anything else returns **true**.

Null

We're dealing with a particular scenario here because there is one single value that has null as a data type: null. Indeed, null is both the value and its type, making it a very specific element of the Sass language.

Note that it has to be lowercase and unquoted for it to be from null type; NULL or any variant containing uppercase letters is from type string:

```
$type: type-of(null); // null
$type: type-of(NULL); // string
$type: type-of('null'); // string
$type: type-of('n' + 'u' + 'LL'); // string
```

null is commonly used to describe an empty value that will be filled later on, or an empty state that's neither true nor false. Because of this, null has a very handy behavior: when evaluated as a CSS value, Sass will omit the declaration altogether:

```
$value: null;

.foo {
   // This declaration will not be output since
```

```
  // the variable is evaluated as `null`
  color: $value;
}
```

While it may seem odd at first, this behavior is actually very helpful when building mixins (see Chapter 4) with optional arguments. Instead of testing each argument to see if it has a value, we can take advantage of a `null` value not being output:

```
@mixin absolute($top: null, $right: null, $bottom: null, $left:
➡ null) {
  position: absolute;
  top: $top;
  right: $right;
  bottom: $bottom;
  left: $left;
}
```

Here's an example:

```
.foo {
  @include absolute($top: 13px, $left: 37px);
}
```

This Sass snippet would be compiled to:

```
.foo {
  position: absolute;
  top: 13px;
  left: 37px;
}
```

Lists

We've just seen the five primary data types of Sass, leaving just lists and maps. These two types are atypical as they mostly act as containers.

Take **lists**, for instance: they are basically what other languages call arrays. **Arrays** are often used to store a collection of related values, usually to iterate over them in order to perform a repeated action.

A Sass list is a collection of zero or more values separated by either spaces or commas. Values from a list can be of any type, including `list`, leading to nested lists (which can be quite complex to deal with later on):

```
$list: (42, hotpink, 'kittens');
```

From there, it is possible—and likely—to iterate over the values from the list in order to perform a task with them, such as outputting similar CSS rule sets. To do so, we need to use a loop (introduced in Chapter 5).

The first point to know about lists is that it's the delimiter (either spaces or commas, known thanks to the `list-separator(..)` function) that makes a list, not the wrapping parentheses. Actually, parentheses are optional unless the list is empty (thus having no apparent delimiter).

```
$empty-list: ();
```

That being said, we highly recommend always using parentheses as they make the code easier to read. Any two or more values separated by a space or a comma form a list:

```
$value: Hello world;
$type: type-of($value); // list
$length: length($value); // 2
$separator: list-separator($value); // space
```

While the previous example might look like a string, it actually is a two-item list (note the `length(..)` function call), because of the space delimiter. To make it an explicit string, wrap it in (single or double) quotes. Here's another—preferred—way of describing the previous list:

```
$value: ('Hello', 'world');
$type: type-of($value); // list
$length: length($value); // 2
$separator: list-separator($value); // comma
```

Although more verbose, it's clear from first glance that the value is indeed a list, and that both values are strings.

While it's possible to call list-related functions on single values (such as `length(..)`, for instance), it does not make the value an actual list:

```
$value: 'foo';
$length: length($value); // 1
$type: type-of($value); // string
```

And since wrapping parentheses do not help to make a value a list, making it (`'foo'`) will also fail. Yet there is a way to create a single item list: Sass allows lists that use a comma as a separator to have a trailing comma after the last value. By adding a trailing comma to any value, Sass coerces it into a list:

```
$value: ('foo',);
$length: length($value); // 1
$type: type-of($value); // list
```

 Lengthy matters

The `length(..)` function returns the length of a value (which might be greater than one for lists and maps), but not the length of a string! To count the number of characters in a string, use `str-length(..)`.

Maps

In some ways, maps are similar to lists. Broadly speaking, a **map** is a series of pairs of associated keys and values where keys are unique to each map. While a list is usually tied to a specific order—as it is basically the only way to find a value within it—a map uses its keys to find their associated value.

In other words, you would use a list when you need an index (for instance, for the `:nth-child(..)` selector), and a map when you need a key (such as a string):

```
$message-themes: (
  'info': deepskyblue,
  'danger': tomato,
```

```
  'warning': gold,
  'confirm': lightgreen,
);
```

From there, you either iterate on the map—in which case you will need a loop, see Chapter 5—or you can pick a specific value from the map based on its key using the map-get(..) function:

```
.message-info    { color: map-get($message-themes, 'info');    }
.message-danger  { color: map-get($message-themes, 'danger');  }
.message-warning { color: map-get($message-themes, 'warning'); }
.message-confirm { color: map-get($message-themes, 'confirm'); }
```

You have to know that in Sass—unlike JavaScript, for instance—keys of a map can be of any type and not just strings. Yes, lists and maps as well, although they have to remain unique:

```
$color-names: (
  #ff0000: 'blood',
  #00ff00: 'grass',
  #0000ff: 'ocean',
);
```

In the previous example, keys are colors. Be aware that using anything other than strings as map keys might confuse developers coming from a background where hash / associative arrays / map keys have to be strings. In my opinion, this is unnecessary and can be avoided by using clean (or *less*) logic and sticking to string keys.

For more information, be sure to have a look at Using Sass Maps[5] by yours truly.

 No Trials with the Trailing Comma

It is possible to add a trailing comma to the last pair of a map. I would indeed recommend doing so as it makes adding new values easier, and git diffs simpler.

---

[5] http://www.sitepoint.com/using-sass-maps/

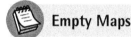

Empty Maps

An empty map is described exactly like an empty list (()). Therefore, when testing the type of the () value with the **type-of(..)** function, it returns **list** (as maps were added to the language later on).

Scope

Now that we've seen what kind of values variables can store, allow me to provide some extra hints about the way variables work, if only for your own sanity.

Variables can be defined absolutely anywhere in a stylesheet: at root level, within CSS rule sets, within mixins, within functions, within **@media** and **@supports** blocks—everywhere. Depending on where a variable is assigned, however, its access might be restricted to a specific code block; this is what we usually call a **scope**.

Sass handles scopes the way you would expect it to: a variable defined in a mixin, function, or rule set is local by default. This means that a global variable and a local variable can share the same name seamlessly: the local will be restricted to its own scope, while the global will be accessible elsewhere in the document.

This is referred to as **variable shadowing** in Sass. When declaring in an inner scope (such as a function or rule set) a variable whose name already exists in the global namespace, the local variable is said to be **shadowing** the global one:

```
$padding: 10px;

.module {
  $padding: 20px;
  padding: $padding; // 20px
}

.foo {
  padding: $padding; // 10px
}
```

In this case, there is a global variable called $padding with a value of 10px. Within the .module {} rule set (scope), a local variable also named $padding is created with a value of 20px. Within the scope, the value of $padding is now 20px, but anywhere else in the document, it still refers to the global value, 10px. Thus, this code snippet will be compiled to:

```
.module {
  padding: 20px;
}

.foo {
  padding: 10px;
}
```

The !global Flag

To definitely override a global variable from a local scope, we use the !global flag. By *definitely*, I mean that the variable is not shadowed but effectively replaced by a new value.

Let's have a look at our previous example using the global flag to update the $padding value, instead of simply shadowing it:

```
$padding: 10px;

.module {
  $padding: 20px !global;
  padding: $padding;
}

.foo {
  padding: $padding;
}
```

Can you guess what the result will be? Have a look at this if you're stuck:

```
.module {
  padding: 20px;
}
```

```
.foo {
  padding: 20px;
}
```

In line four, the `!global` flag actually reassigns the `$padding` variable to the new value, making it 20px for the `.foo {}` rule set as well.

 When Not to Make `!global` a Global Move

While it might be tempting to use the `!global` flag when defining a variable at the root of a document, it is probably wiser to omit it. Indeed, this is an abuse of `!global` that might make the code confusing. On top of that, Sass is likely to prevent the usage of `!global` on a root-level variable assignment in a future version.

The `!default` Flag

Last but not least when it comes to variable assignment is that there's a mechanism that makes it possible to assign a variable if it doesn't have a value yet—the `!default` flag:

```
$padding: 10px;
$padding: 20px !default;

.foo {
  padding: $padding; // 10px
}
```

Because of this, it's recommended that you use `!default` when declaring default configuration variables. Not only does it make it clear that the variable is a default value, it also makes reassigning easier.

The `!default` flag is incredibly useful when building third-party libraries and modules. It enables users to configure the library, but still provide defaults if they don't:

```
// Your configuration of the third party library
$third-party-output-prefix: false;

// The third party library has some default values such as
```

```
// $third-party-output-prefix: true !default;
// In this case, the value is `false` thanks to `!default`.
@import 'third-party-library';
```

The !default flag also comes in handy when dealing with dynamically created Sass files from user input, such as theme files:

```
// User theme stylesheet containing:
// $brand-color: hotpink;
@import 'user-theme';

// Default configuration
$brand-color: grey !default;

.foo {
  color: $brand-color; // hotpink
}
```

Bear in mind that variables with null value are treated as unassigned by default, which means that a variable assignment with !default will override a variable assignment to null:

```
$padding: null;
$padding: 20px !default;

.foo {
  padding: $padding; // 20px
}
```

Interpolation

We are almost done with variables. The last point to grasp is the concept of **interpolation**. Often referred to as **variable interpolation** or **variable substitution**, this concept is not unique to Sass. Actually, you can find it in most languages.

To put it simply, interpolating is the process of evaluating an expression or a string containing one or more variables, yielding a result in which the variables are replaced with their corresponding values in memory.

Let's look at an example. In the section dedicated to understanding strings, we have learned that we can concatenate strings with others. This is useful when building a string from moving parts such as variables:

```
$name: 'Hugo';

.foo {
  content: 'Hello ' + $name + '!'; // Hello Hugo!
}
```

Though, you'll concede that this is highly verbose. Thanks to variable interpolation, we can actually have a string containing variable(s) without having to concatenate several string chunks:

```
$name: 'Hugo';

.foo {
  content: 'Hello #{$name}!';
}
```

By wrapping a variable identifier with #{}, it tells Sass to treat the content of the variable as plain CSS (roughly speaking). One of the most common use cases for interpolating a variable is within the calc(..) CSS function. Let's try it:

```
.main {
  $sidebar-width: 300px;
  width: calc(100% - $sidebar-width); // calc(100% - $sidebar-width)
}
```

Unfortunately, this will fail to work as expected since the resulting CSS will literally be calc(100% - $sidebar-width). Because of the calc(..) function, Sass does not replace the $sidebar-width variable with its value. To prevent this from happening, let's interpolate it:

```
.main {
  $sidebar-width: 300px;
  width: calc(100% - #{$sidebar-width}); // calc(100% - 300px)
}
```

It works perfectly now!

Media queries are another case where you'll have to deal with variable interpolation. To be concise, Sass will only evaluate Sass variables in a media query if they're within a pair of parentheses. So when dynamically creating media blocks, you need to wrap the whole thing in parentheses. This is perfectly fine for complex media queries such as (min-width: 1337px), but it might cause an issue for media keywords such as screen:

```
$media: screen;
$feature: min-width;
$value: 1337px;

@media ($media) and ($feature: $value) {
  // …
}
```

The previous snippet is compiled as:

```
@media (screen) and (min-width: 1337px) {}
```

Yet this is invalid CSS because of (screen). The media keyword should not be wrapped in parentheses. In order to make Sass evaluate the variable, we have no choice but to interpolate it:

```
$media: screen;
$feature: min-width;
$value: 1337px;

@media #{$media} and ($feature: $value) {
  // …
}
```

The last example is for dynamically generated selectors. To use a variable in a selector, we have to interpolate it:

```
$section: 'home';

.section-#{$section} {
  background: transparent;
}
```

For more information about Sass interpolation, be sure to have a look at my tutorial, Everything You Need To Know About Sass Interpolation[6].

Creating Meaningful Variables

Let's face it: being able to use variables to write CSS is awesome. It's convenient, useful and makes our lives easier. Mind, we have to pay attention to keep this feature meaningful, because it turns out to be quite easy to create too many or poorly thought variables.

To finish off this chapter, I will provide some guidelines to creating meaningful variables, serving your project rather than introducing unnecessary complexity.

Let's talk a bit about *naming* your variables. As CSS is a language that is essentially hyphenated (rare ~~exceptions~~ mistakes aside), I recommend that you stick to this convention: use hyphens to separate words within your variables names rather than underscores or *camel case*:

```
// Yep
$brand-color: #BADA55;

// Nope
$brand_color: #BADA55;

// Definitely nope
$brandColor: #BADA55;

// Stop it
$BrandColor: #BADA55;
```

---

[6] http://webdesign.tutsplus.com/tutorials/all-you-ever-need-to-know-about-sass-interpolation--cms-21375

```
// Why are you doing this?
$BrAnDcOlOr: #BADA55;
```

You may have heard of **constants**. A constant is an immutable value that, unlike a variable, cannot be reassigned. Sass does not support actual constants. If you need one—odd, but perhaps understandable if building a framework—I'd probably recommend using uppercase letters separated with underscores (also known as *snakerized*):

```
// This variable contains the list of valid CSS positions.
// It actually is a constant, hence the different naming syntax.
$CSS_POSITIONS: (top, right, bottom, left, center);
```

The variable name should be used to describe the value without explicitly referring to its contents. The rule of thumb is if you cannot change the value (while keeping the same data type) without the variable name becoming meaningless, it is probably a poor name. For example, $spacing-10: 10px is a bad idea because if at some point the spacing changes from 10px, the variable name becomes inconsistent:

```
// Yep
$global-spacing: 10px;

// Nope
$spacing-10: 10px;
```

Keep in mind that you are making *variables*: their value should be able to be changed.

Now there is the case of colors. Unless described with color keywords such as red (unlikely, but just as an example), colors are very hard to comprehend. HSL (Hue Saturation Lightness) notation makes it slightly easier than RGB and hexadecimal, but still, hsl(42, 78%, 54%) is not quite *obvious*.

As a result, it can be useful to store colors in representative variable names. For instance, hsl(42, 78%, 54%) could be stored in a $gold variable since it's a golden yellow. The problem now, though, is that we can only slightly tweak the color without making its name incoherent.

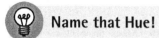 **Name that Hue!**

Name That Color[7] is a crazy little tool that finds a name for any given color.

One solution is to store colors in variables with representative names, and then use these in other generic variables where the original meaning is retained:

```
$gold: hsl(42, 78%, 54%);
$dark-blue: rgb(13, 33, 70);

$primary-theme-color: $gold;
$secondary-theme-color: $dark-blue;
```

Here we store our hard-to-read colors in simple descriptive variables; then use these variables in more generic ones. Now both our code and colors are readable and easy to grasp, and we can still change—and not just tweak—the theme colors without the risk of having incoherent variable names.

It's also best to avoid naming your variables after the way they're used such as $border-color, or $blockquote-margin. While it might sound handy at the time, sooner or later you will use those variables for completely different purposes, and you'll be left with a name that makes little sense, or is misleading even. This is why it's advisable not to be too specific with your variable names.

CSS Custom Properties or Sass Variables

Fairly recently a specification was approved for **CSS custom properties**, often referred to as **CSS variables**. Indeed, custom properties share the same purpose as variables, limiting code repetition by associating values to specific identifiers (variable names). This new feature has already hit some browsers, though we might have to wait a while before it's broad enough to use on a daily basis without risk.

Browser support aside, we can ask ourselves whether CSS variables are here to replace Sass ones. The answer is most likely to be *yes*, although both features share subtle differences that must be understood to have a good overview of the current (and future) situation.

---

[7] http://chir.ag/projects/name-that-color/#BADA55

For starters, there are good reasons why CSS variables are not called *CSS Variables* but *CSS custom properties*. It's because they are not actual variables, strictly speaking. On the other hand, custom properties are very well named: they are *custom* CSS properties. Understand that they are not any different from other CSS properties such as `width` or `color`; only that they are made by authors and not part of any specification—hence the word *custom*.

Before jumping onto what that actually means in regard to Sass variables, let's look at a short example to see how CSS custom properties work. Custom properties must start with two hyphens (`--`) to be recognized as such, and the `var(..)` function has to be used to retrieve their value:

```
/**
 * Declaring a CSS custom property named `main-color` at root level
 * so that it is accessible anywhere in the document
 */
:root {
  --main-color: #BADA55;
}

/**
 * Using the `main-color` variable through the `var(..)` function
 */
body {
  background-color: var(--main-color);
}
```

Now, if you've properly followed everything we said about variables scoping in Sass, you might ask how the `body {}` rule set is able to use the `--main-color` variable, as it's been defined in a totally different rule set (`:root {}`). First, know that `:root` has no special meaning here; we could have used `html` as well. Second, do you remember how the *C* in CSS means *Cascading*? This is for a good reason. The variable is accessible to `body` because it follows the cascade, and `body` happens to be a child of `:root` (the `html` element). And *this* makes a huge difference.

Like most other CSS properties, CSS custom ones do follow the cascade and are accessible to the children of the element to which they've been declared. It is recommended to declare global variables on `:root` because it's the *root* of the document, making those custom properties accessible anywhere in it.

Hence, Sass variables are scoped and rely on a global scope to be accessible any-where, while CSS variables respect the cascade principle and should be defined on the uppermost element to flow down the document. This is the first major difference.

Returning to the previous example, this is actual CSS code parsed and run in the browser, and not compiled in any way. While this might sound irrelevant, it makes a big difference between CSS custom properties and Sass variables. CSS custom properties still exist once in the browser; they still can be read and *updated*—with JavaScript, for instance. Changing a whole color theme might take nothing more than changing the value of a variable on the root element, thanks to CSS custom properties:

```
// Styles from the :root element
var styles = window.getComputedStyle(document.documentElement);
// Get current color set in `--main-color` variable
var color = styles.getPropertyValue('--main-color');
// Replace the color with a new value; now all elements using
// `--main-color` will be updated with the new color value. Handy!
document.documentElement.styles.setProperty('--main-color',
➥ 'hotpink');
```

Variables versus Preprocessors

For more information about the differences between Sass variables and CSS custom properties, be sure to have a look at What CSS Variables Can Do That Preprocessors Can't[8] by Daniel Imms.

Therefore, Sass variables and CSS custom properties both serve the same purpose, but are fundamentally different in their approach. Because CSS custom properties still exist when in the browser, they allow some features that Sass variables will never be able to reach.

Wrapping Things Up

In this chapter we've discussed variables, one of the key Sass features that you'll be using very frequently. As well as running through the available variable types (string, number, color, bool, null, list, and map), we also looked at variable interpol-ation, variable scope, and some best practices around variable naming. We finished

---

[8] http://www.sitepoint.com/css-variables-can-preprocessors-cant/

up with a comparison of CSS custom properties and Sass variables, and when to use each of them. In the next chapter, we're going to discuss functions and mixins.

Functions and Mixins

If you are new to Sass, you've probably heard that it's possible to create your own functions, as well as what's known as mixins. Let's start with what a function is before moving on to mixins.

Functions

In computer science, a **function** is a chunk of code that returns a result, possibly accepting arguments. It's an ideal way to extract repeated pieces of code into a single reusable pattern. As a consequence, functions exist in almost all programming languages, even CSS! Think about it—when writing `url(..)` or `rgba(..)`, we use CSS functions already. What's interesting is that Sass not only provides a lot of built-in functions, it also provides authors with a way to define custom functions:

```
// Using the `darken(..)` built-in Sass function
.foo {
  color: darken(#BADA55, 4.2%); // #B3D643
}
```

In Sass, a function definition starts with `@function`, then the name of the function, then a pair of parentheses—possibly but not necessarily containing parameters passed to the function. The core of the function is then written between braces ({ .. }).

Let's look at a simple example. Here's a function that accepts no argument and returns the base URL for the assets folder as a string:

```
// The `get-base-url()` function has no parameter
@function get-base-url() {
  @return '/assets/';
}

// Usage
.module {
  background-image: url(get-base-url() + 'unicorn.png');
}
```

As you can see, a Sass function returns a result through the @return directive. Note that it must contain at least one return statement, or else an error is thrown. If we'd forgotten the @return statement from our previous function, Sass would have thrown:

```
Function get-base-url finished without @return
```

A function can be defined almost anywhere in a document and not just at root level. When defined within a rule set, a function is scoped to that rule set, the same way variables are local when defined within a specific block. The concept of *global shadowing* applies to functions as well. A local function sharing its name with a global one will shadow the latter inside the scope where it's defined:

```
@function get-base-url(..) {
  @return '/assets/';
}

.module {
  // Shadow `get-base-url()` function within `.module {}`
  @function get-base-url() {
    @return 'http://cdn.example.com/assets/';
  }

  background-image: url(get-base-url() + 'unicorn.png');
}
```

```
.foo {
  background-image: url(get-base-url() + 'kittens.png');
}
```

The compiled CSS of this example looks like this:

```
.module {
  background-image: url('http://cdn.example.com/assets/unicorn.png'
➥);
}

.foo {
  background-image: url('/assets/kittens.png');
}
```

Keep in mind that functions cannot be defined within mixins or other functions.

Parameters

 Parameters and Arguments

A **parameter** is the variable that's part of the function's signature (function declaration). An **argument** is an expression used when calling the function.

As there is little to no interest in using a function in place of a variable when no parameter is involved, let's move on to functions with parameters. These are defined in the function signature as variables, separated with commas. Let's have a look at a (not-so-useful, yet simple) example, a multiplication function:

```
@function multiply($a, $b) {
  @return ($a * $b);
}
```

Parameters can also have a default value—in which case they are called **optional parameters**. To define an optional parameter, do as if you were declaring a variable in the function signature (without the closing semicolon):

```
// `$a` is mandatory and `$b` is optional (default value being 2)
@function multiply($a, $b: 2) {
  @return ($a * $b);
}
```

Note that optional parameters must come after any non-optional parameter. If you try the following, it will throw an error:

```
// Throws an error:
// > `Required argument $b must come before any optional arguments.`
@function multiply($a: 2, $b) {
  @return ($a * $b);
}
```

Before going any further, let's try our new function. When calling a Sass function, you can either pass arguments in the order they are defined, or you can use what we call **named arguments** or **keyword arguments**,[1] in which case you are not entitled to follow the defined order. To use named arguments, do as if you were defining variables in the function call (again, without the closing semicolon):

```
$element-width: 400px;

.foo {
  // Calling `multiply(..)` with arguments in the defined order
  width: multiply($element-width, 3); // 1200px
  // Calling `multiply(..)` relying on default value
  // for second parameter
  padding: multiply(10px); // 20px
}

.bar {
  // Calling `multiply(..)` using keyword arguments
  width: multiply($b: 3, $a: $element-width); // 1200px
}
```

There are three benefits of using named arguments over definition order:

1. They can be declared in any order.
2. Arguments are obvious to understand when named.

---

[1] These are sometimes referred to as *kwargs* in certain languages, but I personally think it makes them sound like a duck.

3. In functions with many optional parameters, only relevant arguments can be defined, leaving the others to their default value.

Here's an example:

```
@function set-color-theme(
  $primary,
  $secondary: darken($primary, 10%),
  $tertiary: lighten($primary, 10%)
) {
  // Do something
}

$color-theme: set-color-theme(hotpink, $tertiary: pink);
```

In this example:

- $primary is passed without being named, simply as a first argument;
- $secondary is left to its default value;
- $tertiary is named and set to pink.

Usage

More often than not, functions are used as CSS values; however, they can be useful in other circumstances. Actually, functions can be used anywhere variables can so within selectors, media queries, properties, values, and inside variables, functions, mixins, and so on. Although, like variables, they might need to be interpolated (see Chapter 3) when used in unconventional places:

```
// Just for the sake of demonstration, here's a function declaration
@function my-function() {
  @return 'foo';
}

// Calling the function in itself does not work and throws an error:
// > `Invalid CSS after "  my-function()": expected "{", was ";"`
.foo {
  my-function();
}

// Calling the function in place of a property works as long as it
// is properly interpolated. See chapter 3.
```

```
.foo {
  #{my-function()}: 'bar';
}

// Calling the function in place of a selector works as long as it
// is properly interpolated. See chapter 3.
.foo, #{my-function()} {
  content: 'bar';
}

// Calling the function inside a variable value works perfectly.
$foo: my-function();

// Calling the function in place of a media query value works
// perfectly.
@media (min-width: my-function()) { .. }

// Calling the function in place of a feature query value works
// perfectly.
@supports (content: my-function()) { .. }
```

Arguments List

Finally, functions can have an unknown number of parameters if ever needed. To do so, simply add an ellipsis (...) to the last parameter of the signature:

```
// `map-deep-get` intends to help getting values
// deeply nested in maps
// The first parameter is the map to browse
// Any parameter after that are keys nested within each others
@function map-deep-get($map, $keys...) {
  @each $key in $keys {
    $map: map-get($map, $key);
  }

  @return $map;
}
```

This type of argument is often referred to as **arg-list** (short for **arguments list**) and is sometimes referred to as *variable arguments*. The name is obviously inspired by the actual type of this variable: arglist (as you can see with type-of(..)). If you read this book in chapter order and just finished the chapter about variables, you might recall that I failed to mention the `arglist` data type. The truth is I wanted to go easy on you to begin with!

`arglist` is in fact a valid Sass data type that only comes up when dealing with arguments lists. As far as I can tell, an `arglist` behaves the same way a list does, so I'm not entirely sure why a distinction between the two was needed. Basically, you can loop on an arguments list the way you would a list, and access its items with the `nth(..)` function the same way:

```
@function dummy($mandatory, $extra-arguments...) {
  // Do something
}

$foo: dummy('Hello', 'how', 'are', 'you', '?');
// -> $mandatory: 'Hello'
// -> $extra-arguments: 'how', 'are', 'you', '?'
```

So why bother adding the ellipsis to make this parameter an arguments list when we could use a regular list? Although this is subjective, I feel it clearly indicates there can be as many arguments as needed—possibly a lot.

There is a specific scenario where I do like using arguments lists: when creating aliases. Let's say you have a function with a long name, such as `ns-get-media-context`:

```
// `ns` stands for namespace, which is usually the short name for
// the app/site/lib.
// Namespacing variables, functions, mixins and placeholders is
// usually a good idea in order to prevent naming conflicts.
@function ns-get-media-context($media, $options) {
  // Do something
}
```

Now, depending on how your code is built, it might be tedious to type the name of this function every time. Consequently, you would prefer a shorter name. So we'll create a `get-context` alias for `ns-get-media-context`:

```
// Alias for `ns-get-media-context`.
@function get-context($arguments...) {
  @return ns-get-media-context($arguments...);
}
```

Instead of repeating the signature of ns-get-media-context, we used a dummy $arguments parameter with an ellipsis indicating that we accept an unknown amount of arguments. If the signature of ns-get-media-context ever changes, there's no need to update the alias!

Arguments lists are much more powerful than simply creating aliases, as they can be used to expand a list or a map of values into a series of arguments passed to a function or mixin. Consider the following $media-context-arguments variable containing the media and the options passed to our ns-get-media-context function:

```
// The first value is the media, the second is the map of options
$media-context-arguments: ('screen', ());
```

If you had to call the function with these arguments, you'd probably do the following:

```
$media-context: get-context(
  nth($media-context-arguments, 1),
  nth($media-context-arguments, 2)
);
```

Using the nth(..) function, we can grab specific values from a list. This example is fine as there are only two arguments, but what if there were four or five? Surely we can do better than this tedious way. Indeed we can, using arguments lists! When calling the function, we can pass our $media-context-arguments list as a series of arguments using ...:

```
$media-context: get-context($media-context-arguments...);
```

In this case, the first argument from the list will be used for the first parameter of the function, the second one for the second parameter, and so on. It's much more concise and definitely more elegant.

This works exactly the same with a map. Let's rewrite our $media-context-arguments variable using a map:

```
$media-context-arguments: (
  'media': 'screen',
  'options': ()
);
```

By naming our map keys exactly like the parameters from the get-context function, we make it possible to pass the map as a series of arguments, where it will *just work*™:

```
$media-context: get-context($media-context-arguments...);
```

Functions for Asset Management: a Case Study

At this point, you know almost everything there is to know about functions—although I must say it's usually quite hard to find a legitimate use case for Sass functions unless you build a framework or complex architecture. As you'll soon discover, mixins are typically much more useful.

One task I do like using functions for, though, is asset management. Let's say we have an assets/ folder containing a subfolder per asset type, such as images/, fonts/, and so on. In order to prevent typing url('assets/images/...') every time we want to refer to an image asset, we can use functions to enhance the CSS url(..) function.

I added SassDoc (see Chapter 10) comments to this example to make it even clearer (and directly usable in your own projects):

```
/// CDN URL where all assets are served from
/// @type String
$base-url: 'http://cdn.example.com/assets/';

/// Native `url(..)` function wrapper
/// @param {String} $base - base URL for the asset
/// @param {String} $type - asset type folder (e.g. `fonts/`)
/// @param {String} $path - asset path
/// @return {Url}
@function asset($base, $type, $path) {
  @return url($base + $type + $path);
}


/// Returns URL to an image based on its path
```

```
/// @param {String} $path - image path
/// @param {String} $base [$base-url] - base URL
/// @return {Url}
@function image($path, $base: $base-url) {
  @return asset($base, 'images/', $path);
}

/// Returns URL to a font based on its path
/// @param {String} $path - font path
/// @param {String} $base [$base-url] - base URL
/// @return {Url}
@function font($path, $base: $base-url) {
  @return asset($base, 'fonts/', $path);
}
```

This very lightweight system is actually a *wrapper* for the url(..) CSS function. Instead of manually typing the whole path in the url(..) function, we can use image(..) and font(..) shortcut functions to make it both more elegant and readable:

```
@font-face {
  font-family: 'My Awesome Font';
  font-weight: normal;
  font-style: normal;
  src: font('my-awesome-font.eot?#iefix') format('embedded-
➥opentype'),
       font('my-awesome-font.woff') format('woff'),
       font('my-awesome-font.woff2') format('woff2'),
       font('my-awesome-font.ttf') format('truetype');
}

.foo {
  background-image: image('kittens.png');
}
```

This code will be compiled to:

```
@font-face {
  font-family: 'My Awesome Font';
  font-weight: normal;
  font-style: normal;
  src: url('http://cdn.example.com/assets/fonts/my-awesome-font.eot?
➥#iefix') format('embedded-opentype'), url('http://cdn.example.com/
```

```
➥assets/fonts/my-awesome-font.woff') format('woff'), url('http://
➥cdn.example.com/assets/fonts/my-awesome-font.woff2') format
➥('woff2'), url('http://cdn.example.com/assets/fonts/my-awesome-
➥font.ttf') format('truetype');
}

.foo {
  background-image: url('http://cdn.example.com/assets/images/
➥kittens.png');
}
```

Native Functions

Sass provides *a lot* of built-in functions to make writing styles an easier task. In the previous chapter, we saw how we could use some functions to manipulate colors such as `lighten(..)` and `darken(..)`, or lists and maps with `length(..)`. This is only the tip of the iceberg.

There are a lot of math, strings, lists, maps, and colors functions that are usable out of the box. Listing them all here would take too much time (and ink!), so if you're interested to know more about the native tools Sass provides, I recommend you have a look at the official documentation[2].

Mixins

Now that you know how functions work, understanding mixins will be a breeze—trust me. Before jumping in, let's see what a mixin actually is.

To put it very simply, a **mixin** is a function that can output code rather than return a result. While a function is a good way to abstract a repeated operation based on parameters, a mixin is a terrific way to abstract repeated style patterns—all with the ability to adapt the output based on parameters.

A mixin can be defined anywhere but inside a function or another mixin. To define it, there's the `@mixin` notation. As for the function declaration, the name of the mixin comes right after it, and then the parameters (if any). Unlike functions, when mixins have no parameters, the parentheses are optional.

---

[2] http://sass-lang.com/documentation/Sass/Script/Functions.html

Let's create our first mixin; a utility to help horizontally center a block element:

```
@mixin center {
    width: 100%;
    max-width: 1180px;
    margin-left: auto;
    margin-right: auto;
}
```

To use a mixin, you have to call it with the `@include` directive (+ symbol in Sass indented syntax) followed by the name of the mixin. If needed, the parameters follow (see the next section):

```
.container {
    @include center;
}
```

When Sass encounters a mixin inclusion, it replaces it with the content of the mixin, replacing the variables with passed-in arguments. Coming back to our previous example, it will yield a result as follows:

```
.container {
    width: 100%;
    max-width: 1180px;
    margin-left: auto;
    margin-right: auto;
}
```

Parameters

Most of the time, mixins will accept parameters since this is where they really kick in. These parameters can have a default value, as we saw with functions. Let's add a little embellishment to this: the default value of a parameter can be the value of another parameter defined before it (this is also true for functions). Like in this example, the default value of the $height parameter is the value of the $width argument:

```
/// Sizing mixin from width and height
/// If height is omitted, same as width
/// @param {Length} $width - element width
```

```
/// @param {Length} $height [$width] - element height
@mixin size($width, $height: $width) {
  width: $width;
  height: $height;
}

// Usage
.foo {
  @include size(100%, 42px);
}

.bar {
  @include size(100px);
}
```

When compiling this code, Sass will render:

```
.foo {
  width: 100%;
  height: 42px;
}

.bar {
  width: 100px;
  height: 100px;
}
```

Inner Content

As mixins behave exactly the same as functions regarding arguments, let's move on
to a feature very specific to mixins: the @content directive.

The @content directive—which has no other form than simply @content—allows
authors to pass block of styles to their mixins. When a mixin has one or more
@content directives defined in its core, it can be given custom content between
braces ({ and }), like so:

```
@mixin my-mixin {
  @content;
}

.foo {
```

```
@include my-mixin {
  // We can add stuff here
}
}
```

As is, this mixin has absolutely no purpose; however, being able to pass dynamic content to a mixin turns out to be very handy when you want to define abstractions relating to the construction of selectors and directives. For instance:

```
@mixin on-event {
  &:hover,
  &:active,
  &:focus {
    @content;
  }
}

.foo {
  color: blue;

  @include on-event {
    color: red;
  }
}
```

In the previous example, we want .foo to be blue, but red when hovered, active or focused. For more information about the selector reference variable (&), please refer to Chapter 6. Anyway, here is the CSS output:

```
.foo {
  color: blue;
}

.foo:hover, .foo:active, .foo:focus {
  color: red;
}
```

As you can see, the @content directive is especially useful when building dynamic selectors or context blocks, such as @media or @supports.

@content Immutability

You store, alter, or iterate the content of a @content directive. What is being passed to a mixin through @content is immutable and unknown.

In addition, variables local to a mixin such as those defined in the mixin signature or the mixin scope cannot be used in passed style blocks. They only exist within the mixin scope and not anywhere else. If you try to use one of those variables in a passed style block, it will either default to the global variable if any, or will simply throw an error:

```
@mixin my-mixin($argument) {
  @content;
}

// Does not work and throws an error
// > `Undefined variable: "$argument".`
.foo {
  @include my-mixin('foo') {
    content: $argument;
  }
}
```

Wrapping Things Up

Mixins and functions are helpful tools to abstract parts of your code in order to avoid repetitions. Both can have parameters—mandatory or optional—if they have a default value. Just remember the difference between the two: a function returns a value, while a mixin outputs CSS code.

Before moving on to the next chapter, allow me to offer you a small example. In the last chapter, we worked on a alert module to display warnings, informative or confirm messages. Unfortunately, we ended up having quite a repetitive code. Perfect case for a mixin then!

```
@mixin message($color, $background-color: lighten($color, 20%)) {
  color: $color;
  background-color: $background-color;
}
```

```scss
.message {
  padding: 10px;
  border: 1px solid currentcolor;
}

.message-info {
  @include message(blue);
}

.message-danger {
  @include message(red);
}

.message-confirm {
  @include message(green);
}
```

Chapter 5

Loops and Conditions

Our journey with Sass is going well so far, don't you think? We now have a solid understanding of variables, and know about functions and mixins.

Mixins and functions usually involve logic to perform well. For instance: "do this in this condition, or do that," or "iterate over this list to perform some action." That's why this chapter will be dedicated to Sass logic handlers: loops and conditions.

Conditional statements represent the simplest control structures, and more often that not, you'll need them to use loops effectively. Therefore we'll start with that right away, *if* you don't mind (see what I did there?).

Conditions

Conditions are a pillar of any piece of software ever written. Even outside of the computer world, we perform actions based on conditions on a daily basis. "If I have time, I'll stop by the cleaner after work," or "I'll have this fancy barbecue regardless of whether it will rain or not." Therefore, it's only logical (pun intended) to have these ***path* switchers** in our programs.

At this point, you might be wondering *why?* Why on earth would we need conditions in our stylesheets? This is a valid concern as Sass conditions are perhaps not something you'll use on a daily basis. Still, when building functions or mixins, it's important to be able to check the given arguments; you may act differently depending on what they are.

In most programming languages, the basic conditional structure exists under the form of *if condition then ... else ....* The syntax in itself depends on the language, but it usually works the same. Sass is no exception, using the `@if` and `@else` directives.

A conditional structure in Sass always starts with the `@if` keyword, directly followed by an expression. This expression can be almost anything: a variable, a function call, a raw value, an equation. The code to be executed if the expression matches lives between an opening and a closing brace (`{..}`):

```
@if $condition {
  // Then do something
}
```

If necessary, we can add an `@else` token and put extra code between braces to execute in case the condition is not matched:

```
@if $condition {
  // Then do something
} @else {
  // Do something else
}
```

 Presentation is Almost Everything

Keep in mind that:

- the condition can be safely wrapped in parentheses (`(..)`) to make it easier to spot and be closer to other languages syntax (such as JavaScript or PHP)

- although not vital, it is recommended that the `@else` directive be placed on the same line as the closing brace to keep a certain visual hierarchy.

Before exploring a few examples, we should understand how Sass evaluates the condition expression to determine which code block to execute. Roughly speaking, it behaves like any other language, converting (or *coercing*) the value to a boolean; if the result is true, the condition is **truthy**, otherwise it's said to be **falsy**.

As we have seen in Chapter 3, only two values are falsy in Sass: false and null. Thus, the conversion to Boolean is extremely simplistic. If the expression is evaluated to either false or null, the @else block is executed (if any). Otherwise the condition is truthy and the @if block is executed (even for values such as 0, " " or ()).

Now that everything is crystal clear, consider the following example. We'll output a specific declaration for old versions of Internet Explorer depending on the status of a boolean variable:

```scss
// Define whether old versions of IE should be supported
$support-ie: true !default;

// If `$support-ie` is truthy, then output the code block
@if $support-ie {
  .clearfix {
    *zoom: 1;
  }
}

.clearfix::after {
  content: '';
  display: table;
  clear: both;
}
```

Multiple Conditions

Life is not all black or all white. Sometimes, there are shades of gray. Sometimes, you need to do it differently, or pull out all stops, and if everything fails eventually you do whatever needs to be done. For instance, "if the weather is good, we'll have a barbecue; otherwise we can go to Miriam's and still cook; or else, I'll stay home."

Sass does provide a way to handle these scenarios. Put simply, you can place extra conditions between the first @if and the optional @else statement. These are written using a combination of both keywords, like so: @else if <condition>.

Tip: A Lesser-known Option

You can also write it as `@elseif` with no space between the two words; however, as very few people know about this, we'd recommend the two words for consistency.

Be aware that as soon as a condition is evaluated to `true`, its code is executed and no other condition in the chain can be matched. Remember that this is basically a switch: in total, either zero or one condition can be matched, not more.

Let's illustrate this with a dummy example, printing a sentence depending on the value of a number:

```
$number: 42;

.foo {
  @if ($number > 1337) {
    content: 'Value is greater than 1337px.';
  } @else if ($number >= 0) {
    content: 'Value is between 0 and 1337.'
  } @else {
    content: 'Value is lower than 0.';
  }
}
```

In this code snippet, our conditional structure allows three outcomes:

1. The value is greater than 1337. This is an explicit statement articulated in the condition expression as `$number > 1337`.
2. The value is between 0 and 1337. This is a partially explicit statement. The condition expression asks for the number to be greater than or equal to 0 with `$number >= 0`, but it says nothing about being lower than 1338. Although we know that if we managed to be lower, it's because the first condition was evaluated to be falsy. Therefore the number is not greater than 1337 at this point. We can then assume that for this condition to match, the number has to be between 0 and 1337.
3. The value is lower than 0. This is an implicit statement as we only used the `@else` directive to imply it. We know that to get there, all previous statements must have failed, so the number is neither greater than 1337 nor between 0 and 1337. Hence, it must be lower than 0.

We could have gone more granular if we needed to. There is no limit to the number of chained conditional statements, although having too many of them conveys a poorly constructed code and is likely to hurt readability and maintainability.

Conditional Operators

All right! Now that we know how to use conditions, we can dive a little further and learn how to express advanced statements composed of several expressions. Think about it: choices do not always rely on a single condition; sometimes it is several conditions that, when all matched, will lead to an event such as "if the weather is good enough and I can find some charcoal, I'll have a barbecue." Then there's the case of at least one condition being true, for example: "if I receive a negative answer, or worse, no answer at all, I'll be disappointed."

You might be familiar with && (logical AND) and || (logical OR) operators from various languages such as JavaScript or PHP. Sass aims to be a human-friendly language, so it provides and and or keywords respectively, which have to be written in lowercase.

The resolution of an expression involving one or many operators behaves like so: each component of the expression is evaluated on its own, then the results of these evaluations interact with the and and or keywords. For instance:

```
$apple: true;
$cherry: false;

// This statement is evaluated as such:
// @if true and false { .. }
// Because `false` isn't a truthy value, the statement doesn't match
@if $apple and $cherry { .. }

// This statement is evaluated as such:
// @if true or false { .. }
// Because `true` is a truthy value, the statement does match
@if $apple or $cherry { .. }
```

Beware when mixing and and or keywords in a single statement. Expressions are evaluated from left to right, and in some cases you might encounter unexpected results. For instance, compare these two identical statements where only the parentheses differ:

```
.foo {
  @if $apple and ($cherry or $orange) {
    color: "$apple must be truthy and either $cherry or $orange (or
➥both) must be truthy.";
  }

  @if ($apple and $cherry) or $orange {
    color: "Both $apple and $cherry, or $orange (or all of them)
➥must be truthy.";
  }
}
```

In the first case, $apple has to be truthy and either $cherry or $orange (or both) must be truthy as well for the condition to match. In the second case, both $apple and $cherry, or $orange (or the three values) must be truthy for the condition to match. Now consider those values:

```
$apple: false;
$cherry: true;
$orange: true;
```

$apple is falsy so the first condition is discarded right away; however, since $orange is truthy, the second condition matches. As you can see, parentheses are not always optional and can have a decisive impact on the outcome of a conditional statement.

Ternary Functions

You might have already heard the expression ternary operator. In computer science, a **ternary operator** takes three arguments, as the name suggest. The first one is usually a condition that is evaluated, depending on whether its result is truthy or falsy; the second or third argument is returned respectively.

Most languages use a syntax borrowed from C, using a question mark (?) after the condition and a colon (:) between the two possible outcomes.

Let's take a JavaScript example to illustrate. In this scenario, we define a background-Color variable to be red if an error variable is truthy, or green if otherwise:

```
var backgroundColor = error ? 'red' : 'green';
```

We now come back to Sass, which is without a ternary operator; however, it does have a **ternary function**. It's basically the same except it's an actual built-in function rather than operator-like syntax. This function is appropriately named `if(..)`.

The first argument of the `if(..)` function is the condition, the second one is the result if the condition is truthy, and the third one is the returned value if the condition is falsy. This function is useful when wanting to shorten an `@if/@else` statement to a single line:

```
$background-color: if($error, red, green);
```

Here, if the `$error` variable is truthy, `$background-color` will be `red`, otherwise it will be `green`. We could have written this using a regular condition as well:

```
$background-color: green;

@if $error {
    $background-color: red;
}
```

Loops

Now that we're comfortable with conditional statements, it's time to address a notion that's slightly more complex. *Loops*, present in many if not most languages, are logical structures that aim to repeat a chunk of code a certain number of times. Loops are typically used to iterate over collections in order to perform a repeated action on all members of the collection. For instance, you could loop over a list of class names to apply a specific color to them.

There are three kind of loops in Sass, just as in any other programming language: the *for-loop*, the *each-loop*, and the *while-loop*. All three are intended to perform an operation for a certain amount of occurrences. It's possible to use any kind of loop in any scenario, although they do have their differences that must be known to pick the right tool for the right job.

The for-loop

The **for-loop** is a logical structure that iterates a given number of times. In Sass (as in any other language), the for-loop expects a starting index and an ending index, and runs as many times as needed from start to end. Inside the content the index variable is provided, making it the ideal ally when wanting to iterate over a set while knowing the current index of iteration.

A for-loop is witten as follows:

1. the @for directive
2. the name of the index variable (usually but not necessarily $i)
3. the keyword from
4. the start index (as a static number, a variable, or a function call)
5. either the keyword through (end index inclusive) or the keyword to (end index exclusive)
6. the end index (as a static number, a variable, or a function call)

Let's look at a few basic examples. First, iterating from 1 *through* 5 (inclusive), then looping from 2 *to* 4 (exclusive):

```
// Using direct numbers and `through`
@for $i from 1 through 5 {
    // Code to execute 5 times, where `$i` equals:
    // 1
    // 2
    // 3
    // 4
    // 5
}

// Using variables and `to`
$start: 2;
$end: 4;

@for $index from $start to $end {
    // Code to execute 2 times, where `$index` equals:
```

```
  // 2
  // 3
}
```

For-loops are especially handy when used with :nth-child(..) and :nth-of-type(..) (as well as the less popular :nth-last-child(..) and :nth-last-of-type(..)) pseudo-classes as they rely on numeric indexes.

For instance, let's imagine that you have a fade-in animation that you apply to all items of a container with an increasing delay to make them appear one after the other. Without a loop, you could end up writing:

```
.item:nth-child(1)  { animation-delay: 0.0s; }
.item:nth-child(2)  { animation-delay: 0.1s; }
.item:nth-child(3)  { animation-delay: 0.2s; }
.item:nth-child(4)  { animation-delay: 0.3s; }
.item:nth-child(5)  { animation-delay: 0.4s; }
.item:nth-child(6)  { animation-delay: 0.5s; }
.item:nth-child(7)  { animation-delay: 0.6s; }
.item:nth-child(8)  { animation-delay: 0.7s; }
.item:nth-child(9)  { animation-delay: 0.8s; }
.item:nth-child(10) { animation-delay: 0.9s; }
```

A bit tedious, isn't it? Especially if you have to update the gap between two arrivals, or the number of items. This is typically where a for-loop can kick in and save the day:

```
@for $i from 1 through 10 {
  .item:nth-child(#{$i}) {
    animation-delay: ($i - 1) * 0.1s;
  }
}
```

Let's go through this piece of code one line at a time to fully understand what is happening. In the first iteration, the value of $i is 1. We open a rule set with .item:nth-child(1) as a selector, to which we apply the animation-delay property. The value for this property is 0s (because, 1 - 1 * 0.1 = 0). Then the $i is increased by 1 and we go through the loop again. This is repeated until $i reaches 10, in which case the loops plays one last time and then stops running.

Note how we need to escape the $i variable (#{$i}) in the pseudo-class to print it correctly as part of the selector. Then, we subtract one to the $i variable (so that there is no delay on the first item) and multiply this with 0.1s to have the correct delay for each item.

Similarly, we could make use of the CSS hsl(..) color function and how it expects a number as a hue. We could apply a slightly different border color (or background color, or whatever) to all items of our list so as to generate a rainbow list:

```
@for $i from 1 through 10 {
  .item:nth-child(#{$i}) {
    border: 1px solid hsl($i * 15, 75%, 75%);
  }
}
```

As in our previous example, the first loop iteration's value of $i is 1. We create the same selector as earlier—.item:nth-child(1)—to which we apply the border property with a value of 1px solid hsl(15, 75%, 75%). Then the loop starts over with $i being incremented by one.

In this case, 15 is really just an arbitrary delta. The first item will have a hue of 15, the second one 30, and so on. As we have ten items, the hue will spread from 15 to 150 (a little less than half the color wheel). Depending on the number of items and the amplitude you want for the rainbow effect, you might increase or decrease this value.

Our last example before moving on to the next loop will be to apply different font sizes to the six levels of headings we have in HTML. We could loop through a list of six sizes and apply them respectively to each level of heading:

```
$sizes: (2em, 1.75em, 1.5em, 1.25em, 1em, 0.75em);

@for $i from 1 through length($sizes) {
  h#{$i} {
    font-size: nth($sizes, $i);
  }
}
```

This code would compile to:

```
h1 { font-size: 2em; }
h2 { font-size: 1.75em; }
h3 { font-size: 1.5em; }
h4 { font-size: 1.25em; }
h5 { font-size: 1em; }
h6 { font-size: 0.75em; }
```

If we want to be a bit more secure, we could make sure that we limit it to six in order not to generate any undesired selector.

To do so, we can use the min(..) function from Sass. In the following scenario, the $sizes list has seven values. We want to loop through the values of the list, but only up to six values. We therefore need to take the minimum number between six and the length of the list as the end index of the loop:

```
$sizes: (2em, 1.75em, 1.5em, 1.25em, 1em, 0.75em, 0.5em); // 7 value
➡s!

@for $i from 1 through min(length($sizes), 6) {
  h#{$i} {
    font-size: nth($sizes, $i);
  }
}
```

The each-loop

The **each-loop** is a logical structure aiming at iterating over a collection, which is either a list or a map in Sass. Therefore, an each-loop runs as many times as the number of elements in a collection (items in a list, key/value pairs in a map). You could imagine a scenario where you store aliases for font sizes in a map such as xs for 0.75em, s for 1em, and so on. By iterating on the map, you could possibly generate selectors to which you would apply a specific font-size value.

There are a few variations of the each-structure, so we will start with the simplest and most popular one: looping through a list. Then we'll slowly move towards iterating over nested lists and maps.

A simple each-loop is written as follows:

1. the @each directive
2. the name of the item variable

3. the keyword `in`

4. the collection to iterate over

As an example, consider the following code aimed at going through the alphabet, one letter after the other. We first define a list of 26 letters. Then we loop through it with an each-loop, accessing the current letter in the loop with `$letter`:

```
$alphabet: (a b c d e f g h i j k l m n o p q r s t u v w x y z);

@each $letter in $alphabet {
  // Do something with `$letter`
}
```

A good use case would be applying a specific background image to a series of elements, such as a photo for each author in a list:

```
$authors: ('hugo', 'miriam');

@each $author in $authors {
  .section-#{$author} {
    background-image: url('/images/authors/#{$author}.jpg');
  }
}
```

Here again, we interpolate the variable to correctly print it as part of a selector. We do the same inside the URL as it lives inside quotes (hence, it would be printed as `$author` without a proper variable interpolation).

In such a scenario, we rely on the image file being named after the class used for the section. This is a fine assumption and way of doing if we actually can name the files the way we want (which is not always the case when using a CMS, for instance).

If we know the filenames but they don't quite match the section names, we can create sublists and rely on what is called the multi-assignment feature from the `@each` directive to rewrite our example.

To put it simply, **multi-assignment** is a feature from Sass each-loops that allows authors to define several variables that can then be accessed in the loop content. It is especially useful when iterating on maps, or, as you'll notice in the next code snippet, nested lists:

```
$authors: (
  ('hugo', 'hugo_giraudel.jpg'),
  ('miriam', 'suzanne-miriam.png')
);

@each $author, $filename in $authors {
  .section-#{$author} {
    background-image: url('/images/authors/#{$filename}');
  }
}
```

In this example, we first define a two-dimensional list where the top level contains authors and the sublists contain everything we need for each author. Then we use multi-assignment in the loop definition to define a variable *per column*. The word "column" is actually fictive here, and only means that the $author variable will serve for the first value of each sublist, and the $filename variable will serve for the second value of each sublist. This code would compile to:

```
.section-hugo {
  background-image: url("/images/authors/hugo_giraudel.jpg");
}

.section-miriam {
  background-image: url("/images/authors/suzanne-miriam.png");
}
```

We are not limited to two-item lists, of course! Let's say we want to have a color per author. Using multi-assignment, it ends up being very easy to do:

```
$authors: (
  ('hugo', 'hugo_giraudel.jpg', deeppink),
  ('miriam', 'suzanne-miriam.png', hotpink)
);

@each $author, $filename, $color in $authors {
  .section-#{$author} {
    background-image: url('/images/authors/#{$filename}');
```

```
    color: $color;
  }
}
```

To add a custom color to each author, we simply add a third item in each author's list, and a third variable in the loop definition. The code would compile like this:

```
.section-hugo {
  background-image: url("/images/authors/hugo_giraudel.jpg");
  color: deeppink;
}

.section-miriam {
  background-image: url("/images/authors/suzanne-miriam.png");
  color: hotpink;
}
```

The problem with this solution is that it quickly becomes unreadable and unmaintainable when there are more than three or four parameters. This usually indicates that it's time to switch to a map. Often, a map is a more robust solution than nested lists as it allows you to name values (the purpose of map keys), making the code easier to read and maintain.

In our current scenario, we actually need a list of maps. This will comprise a list of authors where each author is a map with three key/value pairs: a section name, a filename, and a color. Then, we'll use the map-get(..) function to access individual author properties inside the loop:

```
$authors: (
  (
    'name': 'hugo',
    'filename': 'hugo_giraudel.jpg',
    'color': deeppink
  ),
  (
    'name': 'miriam',
    'filename': 'suzanne-miriam.png',
    'color': hotpink
  )
);
```

```scss
@each $author in $authors {
  $author: map-get($author, 'name');
  $filename: map-get($author, 'filename');
  $color: map-get($author, 'color');

  .section-#{$author} {
    background-image: url('/images/authors/#{$filename}');
    color: $color;
  }
}
```

Here we've started the loop content by storing all properties from the author map in variables, but this, of course, is not required. We could have directly put the map-get(..) calls in the rule set, although it would have made the code slightly harder to read.

Finally, we could also write our code using nested maps instead of nested lists, or a list of maps. In this case, we'd map an author name (e.g. miriam) to a map of properties (filename and color). Then, we'd use the map-specific multi-assignment of the @each directive to iterate over it:

```scss
$authors: (
  'hugo': (
    'filename': 'hugo_giraudel.jpg',
    'color': deeppink
  ),
  'miriam': (
    'filename': 'suzanne-miriam.png',
    'color': hotpink
  )
);

@each $author, $properties in $authors {
  $filename: map-get($properties, 'filename');
  $color: map-get($properties, 'color');

  .section-#{$author} {
    background-image: url('/images/authors/#{$filename}');
```

```
    color: $color;
  }
}
```

When using an each-loop to iterate over a map, the first variable in the loop definition contains the current key, and the second one contains the current value. In this case, $properties contains a map with filename and color keys.

 Two Variables Are Better Than One

When looping through a map with a single variable, it contains the key and the value as a two-item list. This is not ideal, so be sure to always define two variables in the loop: one for the key, one for the value.

The while-loop

The **while-loop** is, as the name suggests, a way to execute a chunk of code as long as a condition remains true. While-loops are frequently used in low levels of software applications, especially to simulate threads, a process that we want to run permanently until there is some form of change.

In Sass, it is very hard to find a decent use case for a while-loop. Both the @each and @for directives cover close to 100% of cases, so it is highly unlikely for you to find a while-loop in a Sass file—unless a library is doing crazy stuff (which should be avoided in a live project).

Nevertheless, here is how a while-loop is described in Sass:

1. the @while directive
2. the matching condition for the loop to keep going

```
$number: 4;

@while ($number > 0) {
  // Do something with `$number`
  $number: $number - 1;
}
```

Take care to ensure that the condition ends up being falsy at some point or you'll get stuck in an infinite loop.

It's difficult to find a single good example for a while-loop in Sass. A not-so-bad one would be to build a `str-replace(..)` function, but it turns out that creating a recursive function[1] is actually easier and just as—if not more—efficient.

Wrapping Things Up

In this chapter, we have learned about two logical structures: conditional statements and loops. Conditional statements are used to execute a block of code based on a condition. Loops are used to repeat a block of code a certain number of times, or to iterate over a collection such as a list or a map.

We can now mix both features—as well as some we've seen in previous chapters—to create powerful helpers. Let's continue on our example from previous chapters by automating slightly further:

```scss
$message-themes: (
  'info': blue,
  'confirm': green,
  'warning': red
);

@mixin message($color, $background-color: null) {
  color: $color;

  @if type-of($color) == 'color' {
    background-color: lighten($color, 20%);
  } @else {
    @warn 'Parameter $color for message mixin should be a color.';
  }
}

.message {
  padding: 10px;
  border: 1px solid currentcolor;
}

@for $theme, $color in $message-themes {
  .message-#{$theme} {
```

---

[1] http://www.sassmeister.com/gist/1b4f2da5527830088e4d

```
    @include message($color);
  }
}
```

In this code snippet, we ensured correct parameters thanks to conditional statements, and automated the CSS output with a configuration map and a loop. Isn't it nice how everything is coming together?

Nesting

If we had to name three features that make Sass a popular stylesheet authoring tool, it would likely be variables, mixins, and nesting. As we will see in this chapter, nesting appears in several forms when it comes to Sass but by far the most popular one is selector nesting. Let's start with this.

Selector Nesting

Selector nesting, or "nested rules[1]" as described in the official documentation, is the ability to write rule sets within other rule sets that result in composed selectors. This is one of those concepts that are hard to describe but surprisingly easy to understand with an example.

Consider two rule sets like so:

```
.container {
  margin: 0 auto;
  max-width: 42em;
  padding: 0 1em;
```

[1] http://sass-lang.com/documentation/file.SASS_REFERENCE.html#nested_rules

```
}

.container p {
  text-indent: 1em;
}
```

This is nothing but plain CSS so there should be no surprise at this point. We could decide to rewrite our code using Sass nesting. Let's try that:

```
.container {
  margin: 0 auto;
  max-width: 42em;
  padding: 0 1em;

  p {
    text-indent: 1em;
  }
}
```

In this scenario, we have inserted our second rule set inside the first. This tells Sass to generate a new selector in descending order from the nested selectors, in this case: .container and p. This piece of code will result in the exact same snippet from earlier.

There are no limits to selector nesting, neither in number nor in depth. You can also nest compound selectors and lists of selectors. For instance, if we wanted to also indent list items, we could add it to our existing p selector:

```
.container {
  margin: 0 auto;
  max-width: 42em;
  padding: 0 1em;

  p, li {
    text-indent: 1em;
  }
}
```

Compiling this would generate the following CSS code:

```
.container {
  margin: 0 auto;
  max-width: 42em;
  padding: 0 1em;
}

.container p,
.container li {
  text-indent: 1em;
}
```

Variable Scoping

We often put selector nesting and **variable scoping** together, and for good reason. Because of the way variables work in Sass, when defining variables inside a rule set, all the nested rule sets will have access to them. Consider our previous example:

```
.container {
  margin: 0 auto;
  max-width: 42em;
  padding: 0 1em;

  p {
    text-indent: 1em;
  }
}
```

Let's assume we want the horizontal padding of the container and the text indentation of paragraphs to be a shared value (here, 1em). A variable is a smart and simple way to do this. Now, depending on where we declare it, its access will be restricted to some selectors and not others.

In the following code snippet, the $rhythm variable is defined at the root level, which means it's available for the entire stylesheet. This includes other (imported / importing) files. That might be what you're after. Or not:

```
$rhythm: 1em;

.container {
  margin: 0 auto;
  max-width: 42em;
```

```
      padding: 0 $rhythm;

    p {
      text-indent: $rhythm;
    }
  }
```

What if we want to restrict $rhythm to the .container selector? We have seen how to do this in the chapter dedicated to variables: we move the variable declaration two lines down:

```
.container {
  $rhythm: 1em;

  margin: 0 auto;
  max-width: 42em;
  padding: 0 $rhythm;

  p {
    text-indent: $rhythm;
  }
}
```

What's nice about this is that the p rule set is still able to access $rhythm because it's been defined in a parent scope. We get the best of both worlds: our variable is scoped to a specific context (not global), and we can use it to share a value between several rule sets. Win-win.

 Global Alert!

Now is probably a good time to remind you of the !global flag visited in Chapter 3.

The Ampersand Selector

Ah, the almighty ampersand selector! It's actually quite an informal nickname for the **parent selector reference**. (You have to admit that's a bit less catchy.)

When nesting rules within each other, it might be useful to dynamically access the parent selector from an inner rule. The & selector does precisely this. Again, it's a tough concept to explain without jumping on a piece of code. Consider a classic link styling:

```
a {
  color: deeppink;
}

a:hover,
a:active {
  color: hotpink;
}
```

How would we handle it if we wanted to nest the second rule set inside the first? It's not really a child per se, more like a state. Let's try something that won't work first, just for the sake of our explanation:

```
a {
  color: deeppink;

  // This is not the selector you are looking for.
  :hover,
  :active {
    color: hotpink
  }
}
```

Can you guess what will be the CSS output for this code sample? It might be a bit tricky if you are unfamiliar with Sass nesting. If you guessed a :hover and a :active with a space, you'd be right! When doing this, Sass treats :hover, :active like children, creating the selector from both parts (a, and :hover, :active) just like before.

So how do we prevent Sass from adding this extra space between a and :hover? We use the ampersand selector to reference the parent selector inside the nested one. Let's see:

```
a {
  color: deeppink;

  &:hover,
  &:active {
```

```
    color: hotpink
  }
}
```

In this extremely simple scenario, & literally represents a once the selectors have been "unfolded". Sass will therefore create the intended CSS, as described at the beginning of this section.

This is, of course, one of the many use cases for the parent selector reference. For instance, if we come back to our paragraph example from earlier, we could also write a rule set for all paragraphs, and then restrict a part of it (with a nested rule set) to paragraphs that live inside a .container:

```
p {
  margin: 1em 0;

  .container & {
    text-indent: 1em;
  }
}
```

Once Sass unfolds all the nested selectors, it ends up with a first selector that is p, and then another that is .container p. As you might have guessed, the & represents p in this scenario.

The & reference is replaced with the parent selector as it appears in the CSS. This means that when dealing with a deeply nested rule, the parent selector will be fully resolved before the & is replaced:

```
.container {
  margin: 0 auto;
  max-width: 42em;
  padding: 0 1em;

  p {
    text-indent: 1em;

    a {
      color: deeppink;

      &:hover,
```

```
            &:active {
                color: hotpink;
            }
        }
    }
}
```

The previous code snippet will be compiled to:

```
.container {
    margin: 0 auto;
    max-width: 42em;
    padding: 0 1em;
}

.container p {
    text-indent: 1em;
}

.container p a {
    color: deeppink;
}

.container p a:hover,
.container p a:active {
    color: hotpink;
}
```

The ampersand selector can also be followed by a suffix that will be added to the parent selector. Consider a scenario where we have a base class—let's say .compon-ent—that is slightly modified when the component is hidden—let's say .component-hidden:

```
.component {
    display: block;

    &-hidden {
```

```
      display: none;
    }
}
```

In this scenario, the resulting selector will not be a selector with several parts. It will be a new class made from the initial one, thanks to the ampersand and the suffix:

```
.component {
  display: block;
}

.component-hidden {
  display: none;
}
```

Context Nesting

There's another type of nesting that happens to be quite popular as well: the ability to nest contexts. The terminology varies in Sass literature, so you might be familiar with this feature as another term. Basically, it's the ability to nest a CSS scoping directive inside another CSS scoping directive or a rule set, such as a media query (@media) or a support query (@supports).

Let's imagine a navigation with items going from block-level display to inline-block after a certain viewport breakpoint. Here's how you would write this in CSS:

```
.navigation li {
  display: block;
}

@media screen and (min-width: 42em) {
  .navigation li {
    display: inline-block;
  }
}
```

The @media directive in itself may vary: some people like to omit the screen and part, but it does not matter much for our example. Now, this does the job very well, but creates a reading rupture between the two rule sets. Yet, they refer to the same set of elements. To avoid this, it is possible to nest the media query inside the initial rule set, like so:

```
.navigation li {
  display: block;

  @media screen and (min-width: 42em) {
    display: inline-block;
  }
}
```

Once compiled, this will result in the exact same CSS code as seen above. Meanwhile, it's an interesting way of writing context-specific styles because it keeps everything related in the same place. In this case, we are still talking about `.navigation li`, just under a different context.

There again, there is no limit to the depth of nesting. It is perfectly possible to nest media contexts within other media contexts. Consider this way of writing our previous code:

```
@media screen {
  .navigation li {
    display: block;

    @media (min-width: 42em) {
      display: inline-block;
    }
  }
}
```

The compiled code is slightly different as the whole rule set has been wrapped in a media context. We will end up with:

```
@media screen {
  .navigation li {
    display: block;
  }
}

@media screen and (min-width: 42em) {
  .navigation li {
```

```
    display: inline-block;
  }
}
```

As you can see, the two nested media queries have been merged to compose a new media query, just like nested selectors do. For the record, the include-media[2] Sass library (see Chapter 10) heavily relies on this feature to handle complex breakpoints.

 Media Queries Support

Some browsers (but not all) support nested media queries out of the box. The ability to nest media queries was not part of CSS 2.1 but came in with CSS Conditional Rules Module Level 3.

As stated before, it works the same with the CSS @supports directive. In case you're unfamiliar with this feature, it basically makes the browser only apply styles passed to the @supports directive when supporting a given set of features. Let's say we want our navigation to use flexbox when supported:

```
.navigation {
  display: block;

  @supports (display: flex) {
    display: flex;
  }
}
```

Just like before, this code will be unfolded. I am sure you can guess the result of the compilation by now:

```
.navigation {
  display: block;
}

@supports (display: flex) {
  .navigation {
```

---

[2] http://include-media.com

```
    display: flex;
  }
}
```

I have to admit it's quite a dull example, but it illustrates well how nice it is to be able to nest support queries inside rule sets in order to preserve selector context.

The @at-root Directive

The @at-root directive was introduced so as to be able to emit a style block at the root of the document, rather than nest it beneath its parent selectors. Admittedly, the use cases for this feature are difficult to come by. Either Sass is clever enough so that we don't have to use it, or the cognitive overhead of a solution involving @at-root is usually not worth the trouble.

Actually, there is one simple yet not that uncommon use case: qualifying a class from within its rule set. Let's say that you style buttons with .button, but want to apply different styles when buttons are links (a elements). You might be tempted to write:

```
.button {
  display: inline-block;

  a& {
    text-decoration: none;
  }
}
```

Unfortunately, this will fail to work, with Sass giving the following error:

```
Invalid CSS after "a": expected "{", was "&" "&" may only be used at
➥ the beginning of a compound selector.
```

When faced with such an error, we can try to interpolate the ampersand selector:

```
.button {
  display: inline-block;

  a#{&} {
```

```
      text-decoration: none;
    }
  }
```

This does prevent the compilation from failing but yields an unexpected result, even though it's quite close to the desired one:

```
.button {
  display: inline-block;
}

.button a.button {
  text-decoration: none;
}
```

To avoid having the a#{&} selector actually nested within the .button rule set, we can make good use of the @at-root directive and have Sass output this rule set at the root of the document:

```
.button {
  color: red;

  @at-root a#{&} {
    color: blue;
  }
}
```

Our final CSS looks like this:

```
.button {
  display: inline-block;
}

a.button {
  text-decoration: none;
}
```

Property Nesting

As stated at the beginning of this chapter, rule sets are not the only thing that can be nested with Sass nesting features. It's also possible to nest properties; however, very few people know this. I suppose this is probably because it's not a super useful feature, but I still feel I should tell you about it.

You know how CSS uses hyphens to delimit words in property names? For instance, take the font-related properties: `font-family`, `font-size`, `font-weight`, `font-style`, amongst others. Well, it turns out that you can nest the second part of each property name inside the first. Hold on, let's illustrate this:

```
.container {
  font-family: 'Jump Start', sans-serif;
  font-size: 42px;
  font-weight: bold;
  font-style: normal;
}
```

We can rewrite our previous rule set this way:

```
.container {
  font: {
    family: 'Jump Start', sans-serif;
    size: 42px;
    weight: bold;
    style: normal;
  };
}
```

If you're like me, you might be wondering about the point of such a feature. Why would you write this rather than the CSS equivalent? I'm not too sure, but it's likely to be remains from the indented syntax era (`.sass`) where it kind of made sense. It might also have some programmatic advantages, such as storing these characteristics in a map.

In the following code sample, we store all the characteristics from our typography in a map, then iterate over it inside the `font` property to generate the correct declarations:

```
.container {
  $font: (
    'family': ('Jump Start', sans-serif),
    'size': 42px,
    'weight': bold,
```

```
    'style': normal,
  );

  font: {
    @each $property, $value in $font {
      #{$property}: $value;
    }
  };
}
```

This seems too over-engineered, if you want my opinion, which leads us to …

Best Practices and Nesting Etiquette

Nesting is a very powerful feature—so much so that there is actually a draft of proposal to bring it (albeit with a different syntax) to CSS itself. That being said, I need to warn you about abusing nesting, especially selector nesting. I've been using Sass for a few years now, and still I have a hard time to justify the use of selector nesting.

Despite what some developers say, selector nesting does not make it any faster to write code, especially when you know your code editor and how to use it. It's unlikely that your speed bottleneck is typing CSS selectors. If you have to use selector nesting, the reason should never be to avoid retyping selectors.

It makes the code harder to read as well. Not only is it easy to lose track of the context when using deeply nested rule sets, sooner or later it's a cry for overly specific selectors. I can't speak for you, but I'd prefer to read a flat CSS file than a horizontal pyramid of rule sets.

Another downside of selector composing (the result of selector nesting), is that it makes the codebase harder to search. Let's say that you're looking for `.container p` because you've spotted a tiny bug in your browser's developer tool. You type this selector into the search engine of your code editor, but it finds nothing. This is because the selector has been generated from the nesting of two rule sets, so you have to actually look for `.container` and then find the occurrence where it contains a p selector.

Here's an example to illustrate the problem. Consider the following markup relying on the Block Element Modifier (BEM) methodology (more on that in Chapter 9):

```
<div class="block">
  <span class="block__element block__element--is-hidden">…</span>
</div>
```

The developer responsible for the styling of this component has heavily used Sass nesting and written this:

```
.block {
  &__element {
    &--is-hidden {
      display: none;
    }
  }
}
```

Let's say that you have to modify this rule to use `opacity` instead of `display`. You cannot search for `.block__element--is-hidden` because this string does not exist per se in the code. As a result, you have to look for all the occurrences of the `--is-hidden` modifier in the codebase. Far from convenient—especially on a large project.

That said, I think this feature still has some positive uses. For instance, being able to nest pseudo-classes, pseudo-elements, and media queries actually is very efficient and good for readability; it makes it easier to figure out that a selector is just a state variation (for example, `:hover`) of the parent one.

It also turns out to be very useful for frameworks / library builders who can compose classes dynamically in a context-aware fashion. Not what you might encounter a lot of in your daily stylesheet, but still a valid use case for this feature.

Wrapping Things Up

Sass nesting is a powerful feature that should not be abused. It could potentially harm readability and maintainability for very little gain.

Try to avoid using unnecessary nesting, keeping it mostly for pseudo-classes, pseudo-elements, and contexts (`@media` and `@supports`) unless you have good reasons to do otherwise.

The @extend Directive

Welcome to the most powerful, dangerous, and controversial feature in the Sass language! The @extend directive is one way to handle inheritance[1] in Sass. The goal is to represent a relationship between two items, where one is a category and the other is an object within that category—sometimes called an "is-a" relationship. Hugo *is a* developer, Chewbacca *is a* Wookie, and a warning *is a* message.

Building Clear Relationships

In order to understand the purpose of @extend, let's start with some plain CSS for a message style, and then more specific info and warning message variations. In our brilliantly designed fantasy, the default message style will give us a basic gray box, while the info and warning variations add some color:

```
.message {
  background-color: gray;
  border: 1px solid black;
  margin: 1em;
}
```

---

[1] https://en.wikipedia.org/wiki/Inheritance_(object-oriented_programming)

```
.info {
  background-color: blue;
  border: 1px solid black;
  margin: 1em;
}

.warning {
  background-color: red;
  border: 1px solid black;
  margin: 1em;
}
```

This code will work fine, but it's repetitive without showing the *relationships* that exist between a message and a warning. We could solve the repetition in several ways, but CSS lacks a way to show relationships *between* classes. You can use multiple classes to show relationships between elements, but the only way to show relations between classes is through selector-grouping:

```
.message, .info, .warning {
  background-color: gray;
  border: 1px solid black;
  margin: 1em;
}

.info {
  background-color: blue;
}

.warning {
  background-color: red;
}
```

We've eliminated the repetition and given some sense of grouping in the initial block—but if those lonely .info and .warning selectors ever become separated from the group, there's no way to know they're related. If our relationships ever span multiple Sass partials (we'll discuss these more in Chapter 9), we're out of luck. The @extend directive provides a shortcut for this kind of selector grouping while making the relationships explicit. We can write the following Sass and output exactly the same CSS as before:

```
.message {
  background-color: gray;
  border: 1px solid black;
  margin: 1em;
}

.info {
  @extend .message;
  background-color: blue;
}

.warning {
  @extend .message;
  background-color: red;
}
```

Extending Utilities

In many ways, @extend looks like a mixin without arguments, and that's another way they're often used. Common utilities such as clearfix and hide-text work fine as mixins, but don't require arguments. Let's use a common Sass variation on the micro clearfix[2] by Nicolas Gallagher:

```
// Mixin Input

@mixin clearfix {
  &::after {
    content: '';
    display: table;
    clear: both;
  }
}

.emory {
  @include clearfix;
}

.gracie {
  @include clearfix;
}
```

---

[2] http://nicolasgallagher.com/micro-clearfix-hack/

```
.miko {
  @include clearfix;
}
```

```
/* Mixin Output */

.emory::after {
  content: '';
  display: table;
  clear: both;
}

.gracie::after {
  content: '';
  display: table;
  clear: both;
}

.miko::after {
  content: '';
  display: table;
  clear: both;
}
```

Using @extend will create less output:

```
// Extends Input

.clearfix::after {
  content: '';
  display: table;
  clear: both;
}

.emory {
  @extend .clearfix;
}

.gracie {
  @extend .clearfix;
}
```

```
.miko {
  @extend .clearfix;
}
```

```
/* Extends Output */

.clearfix::after, .emory::after, .gracie::after, .miko::after {
  content: '';
  display: table;
  clear: both;
}
```

The Placeholder (Extend-only) Selector

To make the @extend output even prettier, we can use a **placeholder selector**—a new selector type that only exists in Sass. Placeholder selectors look like class or id selectors, but they start with % instead of . or #, and disappear completely in the output:

```
// Placeholder Input

%clearfix::after {
  content: '';
  display: table;
  clear: both;
}

.emory {
  @extend .clearfix;
}

.gracie {
  @extend .clearfix;
}

.miko {
  @extend .clearfix;
}
```

```
/* Placeholder Output */

.emory::after, .gracie::after, .miko::after {
```

```
    content: '';
    display: table;
    clear: both;
}
```

This is great for third-party libraries wanting to provide extendable classes without adding bloat to code. If a placeholder is not extended, that code block is never rendered.

Advanced Extending

Extend works by finding every occurrence that matches the original (extended) selector's meaning and adding the new extending selector in its place. It works no matter how complex the selector, what context it's in or how it was written, and what order they are declared. Mixins have to be defined before they're used, but extends do not. These interactions can become quite tricky:

```
.hoverlink {
    @extend a:hover;
}

a {
    &[href*='http://'] {
        &:hover {
            text-decoration: underline;
        }
    }
}
```

Before researching this book, we would never have guessed what that compiles to:

```
a[href*='http://']:hover, [href*='http://'].hoverlink {
    text-decoration: underline;
}
```

Extends will chain together if they become intertwined, which might be powerful but is more often a costly accident. If .warning extends .message, which extends .overlay—then .warning will also extend .overlay by association.

You can also extend multiple selectors in a single block, and even with a single @extend directive. These two .error-message blocks would result in the same output:

```
.error-message {
  @extend .error;
  @extend .message;
}

.error-message {
  @extend .error, .message;
}
```

If you extend something that isn't there, Sass will throw an error:

```
".error-message" failed to @extend ".aliens".
The selector ".aliens" was not found.
Use "@extend .aliens !optional" if the extend should be able to fail.
```

Just like it says, adding !optional to your @extend will silence that error, making your extension optional. This is especially helpful when working with third-party libraries. Here's an example:

```
.error-message {
  @extend .aliens !optional;
}
```

Nesting Extends

The most notorious feature of @extend is when one nested selector extends another:

```
.leonardo .cobb .dicaprio {
  background: blue;
}
```

```
.cillian .fischer .murphy {
  @extend .dicaprio
}
```

If Sass compiled every possible meaning behind that extension—weaving together each possible iteration—the results would be exponentially long. Sass is smarter than that, but still has to cover reasonable possibilities:

```
.leonardo .cobb .dicaprio,
.leonardo .cobb .cillian .fischer .murphy,
.cillian .fischer .leonardo .cobb .murphy {
  background: blue;
}
```

It's a dangerous road to go down, unless you're trying to generate experimental poetry in your CSS.

The Limits of Extending

Extending is a beautiful idea, but there are no guarantees of a happy ending. There are a number of issues that have lead some developers to reject @extends completely. As for the book's authors, while Miriam chooses to be cautious in her condemnations, Hugo's skepticism can be deemed justifiable.

Confusing Cascade

My main complaint is that @extend messes with the cascade[3], changing the specificity of styles in ways that are not obvious or easy to control. While mixins inject code where you call them, @extend injects code somewhere else entirely—adding selectors to the original extended code block, which might be in a different file or even hidden inside a third-party package. While that may not be a big issue for a utility such as clearfix, it can cause major issues when used recklessly. Don't try this at home:

```
%large {
  font-size: 4rem;
}
```

---

[3] http://www.sitepoint.com/web-foundations/cascade/

```
%small {
  font-size: 0.75rem;
}

.message {
  @extend %small;
}

.important {
  @extend %large;
}
```

Which class has a higher specificity, .message or .important? Usually, in a conflict the class defined second will take priority over any preceding classes. In this case it doesn't matter what order we defined the classes, only the order we defined our initial placeholders. No matter how you define your classes later in the document, an extension of %small will never override an extension of %large. The specificity isn't determined by the order in which you use extensions, but the order in which they're defined:

```
.important {
  font-size: 4rem;
}

.message {
  font-size: 0.75rem;
}
```

If there is any chance that specificity will be an issue, @extend should be off the table.

Collateral Damage

Because a selector can appear multiple times in a stylesheet, extended selectors are replaced everywhere they appear. You might be altering code you haven't considered. Using our initial message example, what happens if we want the .message class to look different in other contexts?

```
// in one file...
.message {
  background-color: gray;
  border: 1px solid black;
  margin: 1em;
}

.warning {
  @extend .message;
  background-color: red;
}

// in another file...
.dark-theme {
  .message {
    background-color: black;
  }
}
```

We never explicitly asked for .dark-theme .warning to get a different style, but now there's one that completely overrides the original purpose:

```
.message, .warning {
  background-color: gray;
  border: 1px solid black;
  margin: 1em;
}

.warning {
  background-color: red;
}

.dark-theme .message, .dark-theme .warning {
  background-color: black;
}
```

Many teams avoid this problem by only extending placeholder selectors and only defining placeholders in one location. That's a great rule of thumb, and helps to make extensions clear and controllable.

Hard-to-Read Output

You'll remember that the entire purpose of @extend was to cut down on bloat. In some cases, this can work in your favor, but sometimes it can backfire once you account for gzip[4]—the best practice for serving CSS files. Gzip uses recurring patterns to improve compression. Even though it is clear that our mixin output is larger than our extended output for the clearfix above, various people have reported that mixins can outperform extensions after zipping.

But even before gzip, there's a chance that you're causing unexpected bloat and confusing output. Consider the following bad idea, which tries to extend a bold-text selector:

```
.typography {
  .bold {
    font-weight: bold;
  }
}

.widget-warning strong {
  @extend .bold;
}

.widget-info strong {
  @extend .bold;
}

.alert-error .important {
  @extend .bold;
}
```

This looks great in Sass, but the CSS output is hard to read. You'd want to avoid seeing this in your browser inspector:

```
.typography .bold,
.typography .widget-warning strong,
.widget-warning .typography strong,
.typography .widget-info strong,
.widget-info .typography strong,
.typography .alert-error .important,
```

---

[4] http://www.gzip.org/

```
.alert-error .typography .important {
  font-weight: bold;
}
```

Instead of repeating a relatively short string (`font-weight: bold;`), we've started repeating long selector chains. We've also triggered the nesting feature, which forces Sass to output multiple selector options for each extension. Do we always want `.typography` first in the chain, or do we sometimes want it in the middle? There's no way to state that explicitly, so Sass is designed to cover all the possibilities.

When you see that long list of selectors in your browser inspector, it can be difficult to trace back to your original code—or hard to know your original intention. Suffice it to say, you should look at the output CSS to make sure it means what you intended. But that's true for any feature, `@extend` or otherwise. If you're using a preprocessor, you should be checking the output for unexpected issues.

Media Query Madness

Last but not least, `@extend` fails to work at all across media queries. Selectors inside one media query cannot extend selectors outside that same query (and vice versa). The following will result in an error:

```
%clearfix::after {
  content: '';
  display: table;
  clear: both;
}

@media (min-width: 40em) {
  .container {
    @extend %cleafix;
  }
}
```

Various people have proposed using mixins that will wrap extends, so you can choose between the two options on the fly:

```
// Defining a Mixtend:
@mixin clearfix($mixin: false) {
  @if $mixin {
```

```
      &::after {
        content: '';
        display: table;
        clear: both;
      }
    } @else {
      @extend %clearfix;
    }
}

%clearfix {
  @include clearfix(mixin);
}

// Using a Mixtend:
.container {
  @include clearfix;
}

@media (min-width: 48em) {
  .grid-row {
    @include clearfix(mixin);
  }
}
```

It's a clever solution, but I'm unsure whether it's worth the effort, and hiding @extend inside a mixin might just make it more dangerous. If it's better for your situation, just use a mixin.

Dependable Mixins

While the media query issue may get fixed down the road, the other issues are here to stay. It's nothing to do with how @extend is implemented in Sass; rather it's from basic problems with trying to represent inheritance in CSS. The current hold-up with @media is that every proposal fixing that issue would make the other issues worse.

In the end, we're unwilling to say that @extend is always bad. Many people put it to good use, and you can too. But it's true that mixins are often easier to understand, with little or no downside in most cases.

Wrapping Things Up

We've learned that @extend is one of the most powerful features in Sass, but also that it one of its most controversial. Some developers reject it completely in favor of using mixins, particularly as @extend can lead to issues with the cascade if not used with care, and it can also create hard-to-read and bloated output. In the next chapter, we're going to look at warnings and errors.

Warnings and Errors

Our incredible journey through Sass is slowly coming to an end, and so far you've been doing great! There's one technical chapter left before we look at project architecture, and then you'll be fully equipped to write Sass code in your own projects.

Now we're going to look at warnings and errors. Both form a one-way communication system between the program (in this case, Sass) and the developer (you). If you're wondering about the point of errors in the CSS world, remember that you already know the answer. Whenever you forget a semicolon or use a function incorrectly, Sass throws an error at you, explaining what you've done wrong and how you can fix it, thankfully! It would be a real pain to have to dig into the code to figure out what's gone wrong.

Sass has long provided a way to emit warnings from stylesheets, but it's only recently added support to throw errors as well—and for good reason! Over the last few years, Sass has allowed authors to build complex systems to abstract difficult or repetitive patterns and concepts, such as grids. These systems must be able to communicate with authors, stopping the compilation process with a custom error message if anything ever goes wrong.

Both warnings and errors are emitted in the current output channel. When compiling Sass by hand or by using a tool through a command line interface (CLI) such as Grunt[1] or Gulp[2], the output stream is the console. For tools that include a user interface, such as Codekit[3] or Prepros[4], it's likely that they catch and display warnings and errors as part of their interface. Online playgrounds such as CodePen[5] and SassMeister[6] manage to catch errors but not warnings, so don't be alarmed if you're unable to test them in there.

Warnings

As has been stated, the ability to emit warnings in Sass is not new. It's possible to display messages or the value of any SassScript expression to the standard output stream through the `@warn` directive.

A **warning** has no impact on the compilation process; it does not prevent compiling to pursue or change it in any way. Its only purpose is to display a message in the console.

There are a lot of reasons to use warnings in Sass. Here are a couple, but you're likely to find your own:

- informing the user of an assumption made about the code in order to avoid surprise and hard-to-track bugs
- advising about a deprecated function or mixin as part of a library or framework

Sending a warning is dead simple to do: start with the `@warn` directive, then state whatever it is. Warnings are usually made to provide some information and context, so they often feature a sentence explaining the situation. That being said, you don't have to use a string; you can warn with a number, a list, a map—whatever. Here, we print a string:

---

[1] http://gruntjs.com/
[2] http://gulpjs.com/
[3] https://incident57.com/codekit/
[4] https://prepros.io/
[5] http://codepen.io/
[6] http://sassmeister.com

```
@warn 'Uh-oh, something looks weird.';
```

Using a regular CLI client, this warning will emit the following output:

```
WARNING: Uh-oh, something looks weird.
         on line 1 of /Users/hgiraudel/jump-start-sass/warning.scss
```

Hey, that's nice, isn't it? Although this warning is far from helpful. It says that something looks weird but does not say what, why, or what can be done to stop it from looking weird. We'll discuss how we can improve on warnings further on.

Let's move on to a more serious example now that we know how to use the feature. Imagine we have a Sass custom function that attempts to convert a pixel value in em unit:

```
@function px-to-em($value, $base-font-size: 16px) {
  @return ($value / $base-font-size) * 1em;
}

// Usage
.foo {
  font-size: px-to-em(42px); // 2.625em
}
```

All good. Now, what happens when passing a unitless number—such as 42—to the function? Maybe you've guessed it, but as it's not quite obvious I'll give you the answer:

```
2.625em/px isn't a valid CSS value.
```

This happens because you're trying to perform a calculation between incompatible units (px and em). What we could do to circumvent this issue is assume the unitless value be expressed in pixels and convert it first:

```
@function px-to-em($value, $base-font-size: 16px) {
  @if unitless($value) {
    @warn 'Assuming value `#{$value}` to be in pixels; attempting to
➥ convert it.';
    $value: $value * 1px;
```

```
    }

    @return ($value / $base-font-size) * 1em;
}
```

The function is expecting a value expressed in pixels. We can still make it work with a unitless value; however, we cannot be sure that this is the expected behavior. We can only assume that it's good enough.

Because we're assuming what is the correct behavior for our function, it's important to let the developer know what we're doing and why. Otherwise it could lead to bugs that are hard to track, which is not what you should be aiming for.

Another practical example would be to warn against the usage of a deprecated function or mixin. You might have already heard of or used Bourbon[7], a lightweight mixin library for Sass. Bourbon is actively maintained, and sometimes requires removing helpers from the library. To avoid suddenly breaking a person's code, Bourbon warns about future deprecations way before it actually removes mixins:

```
@mixin inline-block {
  display: inline-block;

  @warn 'The `inline-block` mixin is deprecated and will be removed
➥ in the next major version release.';
}
```

Clever! People who still use the `inline-block` mixin from Bourbon are aware that the library will remove it completely in the next version, so they know to start updating their codebase to remove the mixin.

The Difference between @warn and @debug

You may or may not be familiar with the @debug directive, which prints the value of a SassScript expression to the standard output stream in the same fashion as @warn. You might be wondering why there are two features performing the same task, and what could possibly be the difference between the two.

---

[7] http://bourbon.io/

Well, there are two major differences between warning about a value and debugging a value. The first one is that warnings can be turned off using the `quiet` option. Debugs, on the other hand, will always be printed so that you remember to remove them when you're done using them.

The second difference is that warnings come with a **stack trace**—a report of the active stack frames at a certain point in time during the execution of a program. As a result, you know from where they're being emitted. Debugs only print the value, along with the line they were called in, but they offer no extra information.

The `@debug` directive can really come in handy when you want to know what's inside a variable, for instance:

```
@debug $base-font-size;
```

Errors

Warnings and errors behave fairly similarly in Sass, so learning about errors is going to be a breeze now that you are perfectly familiar with warnings! The only difference between an **error** and a warning is—as you might have guessed—that the error stops the compilation process.

Using errors can be handy when validating parameters from mixins and functions, for instance. In the previous section, this worked even when the given argument was not exactly as expected, but we cannot (and should not) always do this. Most of the time, if arguments are invalid, it is better to throw an error so that the stylesheet author can fix the problem.

You can throw an error using the `@error` directive. As for warnings, you can pass anything to this directive—not necessarily a string, although it usually makes more sense to provide a clear context. The argument (what you give to the `@error` direct-ive) will be printed in the standard output stream, as well as a stack trace to give more insight about the problem. The compilation process will stop immediately.

Let's start with a Gandalf-approved error:

```
@error 'YOUUUUU! SHALL NOT. PASS.';
```

The output might depend on how you compile your stylesheets, as some tools catch and enhance the errors a certain way. Using the standard `sass` Ruby binary (gem), here's how it looks:

```
Error: YOUUUUU! SHALL NOT. PASS.
        on line 1 of /Users/hgiraudel/jump-start-sass/error.scss
  Use --trace for backtrace.
```

With the `trace` option, you can have the full stack trace from Sass itself, which isn't that useful unless there's an actual bug somewhere in the preprocessor. Hence why it is hidden as a default.

 No try/catch in Sass

It's not possible to catch a Sass error in a "programming" fashion, as Sass has no provision for a *try/catch* feature in the way other languages do. Therefore, it's impossible to try an expression that might break, swallow the error, and perform something else instead.

Time to take a look at a *real* practical example. Let's start by writing a small function to help accessing deeply nested values in maps, `map-deep-get(..)`:

```
@function map-deep-get($map, $keys...) {
  @each $key in $keys {
    $map: map-get($map, $key);

    @if (type-of($map) == 'null') {
      @return $map;
    }
  }

  @return $map;
}
```

Let's enhance it with custom errors. But first, consider the following map and `map-deep-get(..)` call:

```scss
$map: (
  'foo': (
    'bar': (
      'baz': 42
    )
  )
);

$value: map-deep-get($map, 'foo', 'bar', 'baz', 'qux');
```

As you may have noticed, the map lacks having a qux key nested in baz. Indeed, baz is not even associated with a map; instead, it is mapped to a number (42). If we try to execute this code, it will yield:

```
Error: 42 is not a map for `map-get`
        on line 1 of /Users/hgiraudel/jump-start-sass/error.scss
```

Sass tries to perform a map-get(..) on 42 and emits an error because it cannot be done. While the error message is correct, it's not very helpful. What would be helpful is to know the name of the key that caused the issue. We can do that!

We already check whether $map is null to perform an early return so as to avoid a compilation error if a key doesn't exist. We can perform a second check to ensure that the map is actually a map, or we throw a meaningful error:

```scss
@function map-deep-get($map, $keys...) {
  @each $key in $keys {
    $map: map-get($map, $key);

    // If `$map` does not contain the next key, return `null`
    @if type-of($map) == 'null' {
      @return $map;
    }

    // If `$map` is not a map, throw an error
    @if type-of($map) != 'map' {
      @error 'Key `#{$key}` is not associated with a map but a
➥#{type-of($map)} (`#{$map}`).';
    }
  }
```

```
    @return $map;
}
```

If we run our previous snippet again, here's the output:

```
Error: Key `baz` is not associated with a map but a number (`42`).
        on line 1 of /Users/hgiraudel/jump-start-sass/error.scss
```

That's much better! It's now easy to fix our map and/or our function call thanks to the helpful error message.

Wrapping Things Up

In this chapter, we learned how we can use Sass to emit warnings and throw errors in the standard output stream. This is usually the console, but it might vary depending on the way one compiles stylesheets.

Warnings are helpful to emit non-critical messages to stylesheet authors—especially for framework and library authors—such as deprecation warnings or code assumptions. On the other hand, errors are used to prevent the compilation from pursuing, making it clear that the code needs to be fixed before going any further.

All in all, warnings and errors are especially useful inside functions and mixins in order to validate user input, ensuring the stylesheets are being compiled as expected.

9

Architecture

Architecture has always been one of the major pain points in CSS development. Without any variables, control directives, macros, or object inheritance, CSS code tends to be long and repetitive—a single ever-growing file. While it's technically possible to split plain CSS into multiple files that reference each other with `@import`, the additional HTTP requests make that a poor solution. As you've seen, Sass has an answer for every piece of the architecture puzzle—but what's the best way to put it all together?

Ask ten experts, and you'll receive ten different answers—most of them involving (or aided by) Sass. OOCSS[1], SMACSS[2], Atomic Design[3], ITCSS[4], and BEM[5] are all popular systems for CSS architecture, but there are many more. If you're using a

---

[1] https://github.com/stubbornella/oocss/wiki
[2] https://smacss.com/
[3] http://patternlab.io/
[4] http://technotif.com/manage-large-css-projects-with-itcss/
[5] https://en.bem.info/

front-end framework such as Bootstrap[6] or Foundation[7], there might be some architectural opinions already built in.

These are all solid systems, none of which were designed with your project in mind. CSS architecture is hard, so it's a mistake to trust any one-size-fits-all solution. There is no "right" answer that works for every team on every project. We'd recommend learning them all, and then mashing together the best parts to create a system that works well for you.

Let's start with a broad discussion of the building blocks, and then look at the ways we can fit them together.

Multiple Files and Folders

Breaking your code into multiple files is one key advantage to using a preprocessor, and forms the basis of any architecture. With Sass, there's no harm in breaking your code into the smallest logical units and organizing it into multiple files and folders. We recommend taking full advantage of it.

Sass has bestowed new power on the CSS `@import` rule, allowing you to combine Sass and CSS files during compilation so they can be sent to the browser as one single file. This is the only place where Sass has stepped on the toes of an existing CSS directive, so it behaves differently in Sass than it did in CSS.

CSS Imports

As mentioned, the CSS `@import` directive allows you to reference one CSS file from another. Importing is handled by the browser and requires additional HTTP requests—since the importing file has to be parsed before the `@import` directive is discovered. If you have a chain of files importing each other, those imports will happen in sequence, blocking the document from rendering until all the CSS has loaded. For that reason, most people avoid CSS imports entirely.

Using CSS imports, you can reference another CSS file using relative or absolute paths, even adding a media query rule for conditional imports. Even though Sass

---

[6] http://getbootstrap.com/
[7] http://foundation.zurb.com/

provides different functionality under the same at-rule, there are various cases in which Sass will fall back to the vanilla CSS output, such as when:

- an imported file has a .css extension
- a filename begins with http:// or https://
- the filename is a url(..) function
- @import has any media queries

The following will compile to standard CSS imports, even in Sass:

```
@import 'relative/styles.css';
@import 'http://absolute.com/styles.css';
@import url('landscape.css') screen and (orientation: landscape);
```

Sass Imports and Partials

Sass imports look similar to CSS imports, but the imported files are compiled into one single output file, as though their contents (including variables, mixins, functions, and placeholders) were copied and pasted into place before compilation. This type of Sass import will only work on files with *.sass* or *.scss* extensions, but you can leave the extension off when importing (as long as there are no similarly named files). In fact, we recommend dropping the extension whenever you can, for simplicity. It's also possible to import multiple files in one command, or import files into a nested context:

```
// Import an explicit file relative to the current directory
@import 'path/to/explicit.scss';

// Import a file with either the .sass or .scss extension
@import 'implicit';

// Import multiple files...
@import 'path/to/emory.scss',
        'miko',
        'path/to/gracie';

// Import a file into a nested context...
// (imagine the file copied and pasted into this context)
```

```
.latte {
  @import 'espresso';
}
```

The most common use of Sass importing is for **partial** files—Sass files that are not compiled on their own but are for importing into other files. If you want a Sass file to remain uncompiled until it's imported, add an underscore (_) to the start of the filename. Sass files that start with _ won't compile on their own, but can be imported into other files. When importing partials, Sass allows you to leave the _ off, which is similar to leaving off an extension. For example:

```
// _authors.scss
.miriam { background: blue; }

// jumpstartsass.scss
@import 'authors'; // Shorthand for importing '_authors.scss'

// jumpstartsass.css (compiled CSS)
.miriam { background: blue; }
```

Running Sass in this directory (sass --update .) compiles **jumpstartsass.scss** to **jumpstartsass.css**; however, it won't create an **_authors.css** file, since it has a leading underscore.

Sass partials form the basis of any Sass architecture. Because all Sass imports are handled at compile time and never interrupt the browser, it's perfectly safe (and recommended) to use as many partials as necessary, compiling them into a single stylesheet for production. For the sake of being organized we recommend breaking out partials liberally, sorting them into folders, and importing them all back into one single master file for compilation. A common Sass directory for a project might look like this:

```
sass/
|
|- config/
|    |- _colors.scss       # Color palettes
|    |- _webfonts.scss     # Webfont information
|    ...                   # Etc.
|
|- layout/
```

```
|     |- _navigation.scss    # Navigation
|     |- _banner.scss        # Site Banner
|     ...                    # Etc.
|
|- modules/
|     |- _calendar.scss      # Calendar widget styles
|     |- _contact.scss       # Contact form styles
|     ...                    # Etc.
|
|- patterns/
|     |- _buttons.scss       # Buttons
|     |- _dropdown.scss      # Dropdown
|     ...                    # Etc.
|
|- main.scss                 # The primary Sass file to be compiled
```

After organizing all your partials, they can be imported into the single primary
main.scss file for compilation:

```
// Primary Sass File: main.scss
@import 'config/colors';
@import 'config/webfonts';

@import 'patterns/buttons';
@import 'patterns/dropdown';

@import 'layout/navigation';
@import 'layout/banner';

@import 'modules/calendar';
@import 'modules/contact';
```

Components and Organization

We've advised you to use partials, folders, and imports—but what's really important
is how to use them efficiently. This is where everyone's opinions differ, and your
mileage may vary.

Most CSS and Sass organization systems are based on some concept of user interface
"components" or discrete pieces that can be put together to form a complete project.
Components can be any size or shape, but they should focus on doing one task in-
dependently, and in a reusable way. A button, a drop-down, a calendar, and a search

form are all examples of components that can be reused at different places across a project. Thinking about your project as a collection of components will help you towards having an organized and maintainable architecture, whether you're using Sass or plain CSS.

Because of the way CSS works, the order of your code will also affect its meaning: later code has priority in the cascade over the code before it. Some of the popular branded architectures (the ones you know by name) try to eliminate this feature of the cascade entirely, but I use it as a guide—organizing code from the most general to the most specific—so the priority override makes sense. Code that we want applied generally across the site should come first, growing slowly in specificity and detail as we move towards more unique components and special cases.

I first learned of this approach from Natalie Downe[8]'s wonderful CSS Systems[9] talk in 2008 before I'd ever used Sass. Her architecture at the time started with elements (h1, ol, ul, and so on) grouped by "type", followed by classes grouped by the "effect" created, and finally IDs grouped by the "component" they affect. These days it's common practice to avoid IDs altogether, and break elements into smaller pieces, but the concept remains the same: global defaults first, followed by site-wide patterns and broad layouts, and finally, more specific modules, themes, and overrides.

Sass projects include another category of site-wide defaults not found in CSS: code with no output at all—such as variables, functions, and mixin definitions. Many people (myself included) break that code into its own set of partials, to be imported anywhere it might be useful. I have a complete folder just for site-wide Sass helpers and configuration that don't result in output. Those files act as a single, definitive, and reusable configuration that defines the boundaries of a project. By ensuring your configuration is output-free, you can import it anywhere without worrying about duplicated or unwanted styles.

Here are some guidelines for thinking about architecture:

1. Break your code into the smallest logical component partials.
2. Organize your partials into grouped folders based on specificity.
3. Import those partials into one master file in order of specificity.

---

[8] https://twitter.com/Natbat
[9] http://www.slideshare.net/nataliedowne/css-systems-presentation

However, many variations do exist on the specific ways people implement those ideas.

You may also find that a lot of the branded systems developed by and for massive companies with large-scale needs don't always translate to smaller teams and products. Every project has different requirements, so you should never assume that the best solution for InstaFace or MyPinBook is going to be the best solution for you.

Object-oriented CSS (OOCSS)

OOCSS[10] is one of the original front-end architectures, and the initial inspiration for adding the @extend directive to Sass. A project from Nicole Sullivan[11], it places a strong emphasis on finding the right *granularity* for CSS objects, a theme that comes up in most of the systems we'll look at here.

Sullivan argues that rather than trying to match back-end objects, a CSS object should look for more granular design patterns that might be used across a variety of content types. A prime example is what she calls the **media object**—a fixed-size media element (such as an image or video) alongside fluid content such as text.

---

[10] https://github.com/stubbornella/oocss/wiki
[11] https://twitter.com/stubbornella

Figure 9.1. Facebook media object

If you look at Facebook, which Sullivan helped refactor, you'll see one media-object design used across the site to display a wide range of back-end objects—from stories and comments, to notifications, advertisements, and profile details. You can see an example in Figure 9.1. By defining objects at a granular level, a small amount of CSS can be used to style large swathes of the application.

At its best, OOCSS is a powerful tool for simplifying CSS and perfecting the performance of large-scale applications. But taken to extremes, the OOCSS approach can leave you with a mess of single-purpose utility classes (such as `.padding-left-10px`) that couple your HTML and CSS too tightly, and eliminate any maintainability you might get from more semantic code. You'll have to find the right balance for each project.

Whatever else you do, the two main principles of OOCSS are worth keeping in mind (indeed, committing to memory) while you work out your own architecture:

▨ **Separate structure and skin.** By having multiple design skins (colors, backgrounds, borders, and so on) that you can mix and match with structural objects, it's possible to achieve more visual variety with less code. In practice, this also means decoupling styles from the base semantics of HTML tags. By styling classes (`.primary-header`) instead of tags (`h1`), you have more flexibility to keep HTML meaningful, while applying consistent styles wherever they're appropriate.

▨ **Separate container and content.** OOCSS objects should not be dependent on their location or context, but be reusable and able to fill whatever container they are given. This ensures that an object will look the same in any context, without developers having to guess what a given element or class will do in different situations.

There is no organizational structure built into OOCSS, but there is a framework available on GitHub[12] that provides a number of common objects, as well as documentation on customizing the framework to your needs.

Atomic Design

Atomic Design[13] is also driven by questions of granularity. Initially devised by Brad Frost[14], an atomic project is broken down into five stages: atoms, molecules, organisms, templates, and pages. The idea is to style the stages in order, starting granular and working outwards, with each stage building on the one before.

According to Atomic Design, **atoms** can be abstract information such as color palettes, fonts, and typographic scales; they can also be default styles for tags such as form labels, buttons, and paragraphs. Since I can never remember the scientific terms, I break these two ideas down further and refer to the former as "configuration" or "settings" (having no output on their own), and the latter "base" or "initial" styles (having output).

Atoms can be put together to form **molecules**. Combine an image with a paragraph and button (all atoms), and you have a simple product-listing molecule. Molecules are small components that do one task well. Group a number of these molecules together, and you have an **organism** (in this case, a gallery of products). Organisms

---

[12] https://github.com/stubbornella/oocss
[13] http://patternlab.io/
[14] https://twitter.com/brad_frost

are larger grouped components that form a section of the interface. Your site banner might also be an organism, combining a logo, navigation, and search form. I call these next two stages "patterns" and "components," but it's recommended that you work with your team to find terms you all understand clearly.

At this point, the developers of Atomic Design abandon their biochemical analogy, and move to *templates*. Templates combine the smaller molecules and organisms into actual layout structures. If you run a news site, you might have a list template and a detail template for your articles. Each specific instance of a template is called a *page*. The home page and archive page of your news site may both use the article-list template, but they have different content. Pages are the most specific combination of all the other stages.

A standard Atomic Design directory will be organized into these five stage-based folders:

```
sass/
|
|- atoms/
|    |- _colors.scss
|    |- _buttons.scss
|    ...
|
|- molecules/
|    |- _navigation.scss
|    |- _search.scss
|    ...
|
|- organisms/
|    |- _banner.scss
|    |- _gallery.scss
|    ...
|
|- templates/
|    |- _list.scss
|    |- _detail.scss
|    ...
|
|- pages/
|    |- _home.scss
|    |- _archive.scss
```

```
|    ...
|
|- main.scss
```

Atomic Design also provides a framework called Pattern Lab[15]. As with OOCSS, avoid confusing the framework with the design system philosophy. You can apply the philosophy anywhere, but the tools are still available if you need them. Frameworks can be a great way to keep code consistent across a large team or project, but always remember that you know your project better than Brad Frost, Nicole Sullivan, or the authors of this book. If there's a conflict between your needs and the framework you're using, always put your project first.

Block, Element, Modifier (BEM)

BEM[16] is a system developed by the Yandex[17] team. This is a much more extensive system, with its fingers in every aspect of your code—from JSON data structures, to templates, as well as CSS.

The BEM CSS architecture is built around the three ideas in its title. **Blocks** are components of any size, and can be nested inside each other. The `header` block might contain a `logo` block, a `navigation` block, and a `search` block. Blocks are reusable, independent, and mobile—so they can be put anywhere on the page, and repeated as often as necessary. **Elements** are the constituent parts that belong to a specific block. A `menu` block might be made up of four `tab` elements. **Modifiers** are flags on blocks or elements that change their appearance, behavior, or state.

The most immediately recognizable aspect of BEM syntax is an intricate naming convention that uses long class names instead of nesting selectors. Rather than targeting `.block .element`, you would target `.block__element`. There are variations on the exact syntax, but the formal documentation allow hyphens (-) within a block, element, or modifier name; double underscore (__) between block and element names; and single underscore (_) before a boolean (true/false) modifier, or between a key-value modifier name and its given value.

---

[15] http://patternlab.io/

[16] https://en.bem.info/

[17] https://www.yandex.com/

Here's an example straight from the BEM documentation that defines a `form` block with a `_login` boolean modifier, a `_theme_forest` key-value modifier, and two elements:

```
<form class="form form_login form_theme_forest">
  <input class="form__input">
  <input class="form__submit form__submit_disabled">
</form>
```

A related Sass partial would look like this:

```
.form {}
.form_theme_forest {}
.form_login {}
.form__input {}
.form__submit {}
.form__submit_disabled {}
```

When BEM naming became popular, people started using the Sass parent selector (&) to automatically generate their BEM class names with less repetition in the code:

```
.form {
  border: 1px solid black;

  &__submit {
    background-color: green;

    &_disabled {
      background-color: gray;
    }
  }
}
```

```
.form {
  border: 1px solid black;
}
.form__submit {
  background-color: green;
}
```

```
.form__submit_disabled {
  background-color: gray;
}
```

On the surface, this works great—but it comes at the cost of searchability, as was pointed out in Chapter 6. If another developer has to find the `.form__submit_dis-abled` Sass in order to make a change, searching your Sass files for `.form__sub-mit_disabled` will fail to return any results.

The BEM file structure goes beyond CSS and Sass, organizing all assets (JavaScript, CSS, images, and so on) into shared directories by block. Elements and modifiers have their own subdirectories using the same underscore-driven naming conventions:

```
blocks/
|- input/
|   |- _type/
|   |   |- input_type_search.css
|   |
|   |- __box/
|   |   |- input__box.css
|   |
|   |- input.css
|   |- input.js
|
|- button/
|   |- button.css
|   |- button.js
|   |- button.png
```

Scalable and Modular Architecture for CSS (SMACSS)

SMACSS[18] is a book, workshop, and philosophy by Jonathan Snook[19]. Like Atomic Design, this architecture uses five categories for organizing your CSS, except that they aren't organized from small to large. Detailed naming patterns are provided to help keep class names consistent. It's one of the most popular brand-name architectures, and may even be the most comprehensive.

---

[18] https://smacss.com/
[19] https://twitter.com/snookca

The five categories here are base, layout, module, state, and theme. **Base** rules define the default style of elements, which work similarly to the atoms of Atomic Design. **Layout** styles are used to break the document into sections that can contain **modules**, the individual components of a design. **State** rules define different JavaScript-dependent states for a module or layout; that is, how does it change when it is active or inactive, collapsed or expanded? Most sites have no need for **themes**, but they can be used to describe multiple style options for the same modules.

In order to help keep CSS and HTML modules small and mobile, SMACSS pays special attention to what Snook calls the *depth of applicability*. You may know of the Sass "inception rule," which states that you should never nest selectors more than three layers deep. That rule helps to keep selectors short (no more than three layers), but the depth of applicability is a bit different. Rather than counting the number of layers, it counts the *total DOM distance* between the first and last layers.

Let's look at a simple example. Since `.mammalia > .primates > .hominidae > .sapiens > .rollsman > .erin` has a depth of six, the same basic selector written as `.mammalia .sapiens .erin` would still have a depth of six. By shortening the selector, we've lowered the specificity (a good thing!), but we still have a large depth of applicability. The problem with so much depth is that it makes our CSS more dependent on a particular HTML structure. This is generally solved by keeping our HTML and CSS components small and independent from their containers.

Hugo's 7–1

Hugo uses a variation of SMACSS for organizing Sass partials. He calls it the "7-1[20]" system, because it uses seven folders of partials and one master file to pull them all together.

The **base/** folder contains broad standards across a site—such as a reset, default styles for common HTML tags, common animations, and basic typography. The **layout** folder includes everything one might need for laying out the structure of a site; for example, boilerplate-like headers, footers, and navigation, as well as your grid system and layout helpers. The **components** folder is organized into partials by component; the **pages** folder contains any page-specific styles; and a `themes` folder holds any theme-related styles (if your project has multiple themes).

---

[20] http://sass-guidelin.es/#the-7-1-pattern

7-1 also includes an **abstracts** folder for Sass tools and helpers, which is organized into partials for global variables, functions, mixins, and placeholders. Nothing in this folder should output any CSS if compiled on its own.

Hugo leaves the possibility of organizing these partials by topic (typography, colors, etc.) rather than type (variables, mixins, functions) for larger projects, but I recommend that across the board. The topic is always the more important distinction in my mind. Placeholders are the only type that I treat in any special way, because their output remains in the location they are defined—while variables, functions, and mixins create output where they are used.

Finally, there is a **vendors** folder for third-party libraries, frameworks, and toolkits such as Normalize, Bootstrap, jQueryUI, FancyButtonsOMG, and so on. These are often kept separate so as to not edit them should they need upgrading later.

Put it all together, and you have a Sass directory similar to this:

```
sass/
|
|- base/
|    |- _reset.scss         # Reset/normalize
|    |- _typography.scss    # Typography rules
|    ...                    # Etc.
|
|- components/
|    |- _buttons.scss       # Buttons
|    |- _carousel.scss      # Carousel
|    |- _cover.scss         # Cover
|    |- _dropdown.scss      # Dropdown
|    ...                    # Etc.
|
|- layout/
|    |- _navigation.scss    # Navigation
|    |- _grid.scss          # Grid system
|    |- _header.scss        # Header
|    |- _footer.scss        # Footer
|    ...                    # Etc.
|
|- pages/
|    |- _home.scss          # Home specific styles
|    |- _contact.scss       # Contact specific styles
|    ...                    # Etc.
|
```

```
|- themes/
|    |- _theme.scss         # Default theme
|    |- _admin.scss         # Admin theme
|    ...                    # Etc.
|
|- utils/
|    |- _variables.scss     # Sass Variables
|    |- _functions.scss     # Sass Functions
|    |- _mixins.scss        # Sass Mixins
|    |- _helpers.scss       # Class & placeholders helpers
|
|- vendors/
|    |- _bootstrap.scss     # Bootstrap
|    |- _jquery-ui.scss     # jQuery UI
|    ...                    # Etc.
|
`- main.scss               # Main Sass file
```

Inverted Triangle CSS (ITCSS)

ITCSS[21] is a new architecture that is just starting to gain attention. This system from Harry Roberts[22] does a great job defining the problem of CSS architecture and proposing a solution that comes directly out of the CSS language. Rather than working *around* inheritance and specificity, Roberts puts them at the center of his methodology.

ITCSS organizes all your Sass and CSS based on three metrics: reach, specificity, and explicitness—visualized as an inverted triangle, as shown in Figure 9.2:

---

[21] http://technotif.com/manage-large-css-projects-with-itcss/
[22] https://twitter.com/csswizardry

Figure 9.2. ITCSS's inverted triangle

Code should be organized from least to most *explicit*, starting with general catch-all rules (such as a reset) and moving up to more explicit styles (such as `.contact-form`). Similarly, code is organized from broadest to narrowest *reach*—so that styles affecting more HTML come early in the code, and styles with a more localized application come later. Finally, code is organized from lowest to highest *specificity*, so that later code can always override earlier code.

With those metrics in mind, the triangle is broken down into seven layers. Each layer is more specific, explicit, and narrow-reaching than the layer before it, as shown in Figure 9.3:

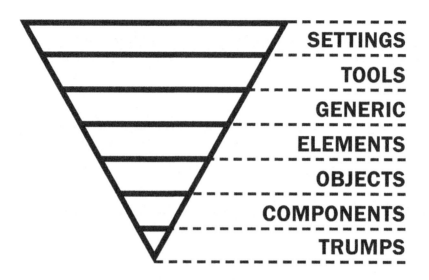

Figure 9.3. ITCSS's layers

Let's explore what these layers are in detail. **Settings** contains global Sass configuration that can be accessed anywhere in the project, such as font sizes, colors, and other project configuration. **Tools** are global functions and mixins that are helpful across the project and not specific to one component. **Generic** is the first layer with CSS output of its own, which includes browser resets or normalization, global box-sizing, and any other broad-scoped rules. The **elements** layer provides default styles for bare HTML elements such as links and paragraphs. It's similar to the generic layer, except that it provides a more opinionated style.

ITCSS **objects** are similar to OOCSS objects, and are defined in class-based selectors. They define reusable patterns that have a consistent structure no matter what content or cosmetic style is applied, just like the OOCSS media object does. **Components** are recognizable pieces of an interface, such as a contact form or a product listing. After the initial setup, this is where the majority of a project's feature-building work takes place. Finally, **trump** styles can be used to override any other layer. Trumps should be used sparingly, and have as narrow a scope as possible.

All these layers can be organized into groups of partials. Roberts uses a multilevel file-naming convention (`layer-name.partial-name.scss`), but we'd recommend using folders instead. The results could look like this:

```
@import "settings/global";
@import "settings/colors";

@import "tools/functions";
@import "tools/mixins";

@import "generic/box-sizing";
@import "generic/normalize";

@import "elements/headings";
@import "elements/links";

@import "objects/wrappers";
@import "objects/grid";

@import "components/site-nav";
@import "components/buttons";
@import "components/carousel";

@import "trumps/clearfix";
@import "trumps/utilities";
@import "trumps/ie8";
```

Miriam's Mix-n-Match

All that is well and good, but I'm writing this chapter and I think my own architecture is way cooler than anything else we've discussed. I'm yet to give it a name, but I will as soon as I decide to tour the universe giving workshops to all my adoring fans. A girl can dream, right?

To tell you the truth, I love parts of all these systems—especially ITCSS. I take what works for my team, and make adjustments as needed from one project to the next. For me, it all starts with one rule: follow the cascade. In practice it looks a lot like ITCSS or Atomic Design (though I find the latter's biochemical metaphor confusing). I use the same metrics, but break down the categories in slightly different ways.

I start with Sass config files that have no output but define all the parameters of a design: colors, fonts, sizes, media-queries, z-indexes, and so on. In my case, it's almost entirely Sass map variables accessed with a powerful set of functions and mixins I take from project to project: OddBird's[23] Accoutrement toolkits. Chris Sauvé[24] refers to this approach as a "Sass Central Nervous System"—a consistent system for maintaining and accessing abstract meta-patterns and style guidelines. Ours look something like this:

```scss
// Accoutrement Config
// -------------------

$colors: (
  // base color palette
  'brand-blue': hsl(195, 100%, 43%),
  'brand-red': hsl(0, 100%, 50%),
  'brand-pink': hsl(330, 100%, 45%),

  // color style guide
  'background': hsl(0, 0%, 100%),
  'text': 'brand-blue' ('shade': 80%),
  'action': 'brand-pink',
  'focus': 'brand-blue',
);

$sizes: (
  // base font size
  'body-text': 22px,

  // type sizes
  'rhythm': 'body-text' ('minor-third': 2),
  'h1': 'body-text' ('minor-third': 3),
  'h2': 'body-text' ('minor-third': 2),
  'h3': 'body-text' ('minor-third': 1),

  // other
  'corners': 3px,
  'page': 30rem,
);

$fonts: (
  // hosted web font
  'body': (
    'name': 'CenturyOldStyle',
```

---

[23] https://github.com/oddbird
[24] https://twitter.com/lemonmade

```
      'stack': ('Baskerville', 'Palatino', 'Cambria', 'Georgia',
⇥ 'serif'),
      'regular': 'CenturyOldStyle-regular', // webfont file names...
      'italic': 'CenturyOldStyle-italic',
      'bold': 'CenturyOldStyle-bold',
   ),

   // web-safe font stack
   'code': (
      'name': 'Consolas',
      'stack': ('Menlo', 'Monaco', 'Lucida Console', 'Liberation Mono'
⇥, 'DejaVu Sans Mono', 'Bitstream Vera Sans Mono', 'Courier New',
⇥'monospace', 'serif')
   ),
);
```

The **toolkit** layer is prebuilt, and moves with us from project to project. It includes functions and mixins that put our configuration to work: automating `@font-face` imports, font-stacks, and typographical rhythms, as well as applying our color palette. It also helps with accessible color contrasts, and automatically generates a visual style guide, so we can see the fonts, colors, and sizes in action.

The next level up is what I call **initial** styles—resets, web font imports, global defaults, and so on. This is the first layer of code with actual CSS output, and it's a thin layer. At this point we're not styling any real patterns, just trying to establish a slightly more beautiful and branded version of the browser defaults.

From there I often establish the site **layout**, adding patterns as needed. The layout partials are similar to Hugo's, describing all the primary structures of the site. **Patterns** are design objects, similar to objects in OOCSS and ITCSS. They're not related to specific content, and might be used anywhere, for anything. For example, buttons and form elements are always some of my first design patterns on a project.

Patterns are abstract, and have no real meaning until they're used in a **component**—the actual bits of user interface that appear on a site. Components should follow all the rules described earlier in the chapter: reusable, repeatable, and able to fit in any container. What others systems call page and theme styles are usually defined either as layout templates or components that just happen to be full screen. Any vendor code that I use will come through a packaging system such as npm, and live outside my visible Sass directory:

```
sass/
|
|- config/
|    |- _colors.scss       # Color palettes
|    |- _fonts.scss        # Font palettes
|    ...                   # Etc.
|
|- initial/
|    |- _init.scss         # reset/normalization
|    |- _root.scss         # global defaults (mostly :root, html, body)
|    |- _webfonts.scss     # @font-face imports
|    ...                   # Etc.
|
|- layout/
|    |- _navigation.scss   # Navigation
|    |- _banner.scss       # Site Banner
|    ...                   # Etc.
|
|- patterns/
|    |- _buttons.scss      # Buttons
|    |- _dropdown.scss     # Dropdown
|    ...                   # Etc.
|
|- components/
|    |- _calendar.scss     # Calendar widget styles
|    |- _contact.scss      # Contact form styles
|    ...                   # Etc.
|
|- main.scss              # The primary Sass file to be compiled
```

Lately, I've also included a **styleguide** folder, and an extra `styleguide.scss` root Sass file to be compiled separately. These files contain any styleguide-specific components not required by the main app—styles for the color palette, font specimens, and so on.

Modular Imports in Sass 4

As this chapter was being written, the core Sass designers, Natalie Weizenbaum and Chris Eppstein, were working out the details for **modular imports**, the major new feature that is driving plans for Sass 4. The specifics are still in flux, but the direction they're going in is exciting, so it's worth giving you a sneak peak at what they've done so far.

Modular imports are a move away from the CSS @import syntax towards one that is more powerful and Sass-specific. Where Sass imports currently work as though the entire imported document has been cut and pasted into place, modular imports provide a lot more control for the developer—inspired by best practice in languages such as Python and Dart. It will probably look a little like this:

```
@use 'path/to/sitepoint/author' as 'miriam';

.sitepoint {
  @include miriam.write('Jump Start Sass');
  -webkit-paycheck: miriam.money('millions');
}
```

Okay, there may not be a -webkit-paycheck property coming anytime soon, but the rest looks good. So what's it all about, and why do we need it?

Locality

With the current Sass import system, variables, mixins, and functions live in a global namespace across all files; conflicts are common. It's impossible to tell by looking at a single Sass file what already exists in that global space; however, with modular imports, nothing is made global unless I explicitly request it. The @use directive will be visible at the top of any importing file, giving me a complete list of available APIs and the power to namespace each however I see fit.

If you @use 'example/grids' as 'grid' at the top of a file, and the **example/grids.scss** file contains a span() mixin and a gutter() function, then they become available in your file as grid.span() and grid.gutter() (the . syntax is still under discussion). The same will be possible with variables, so a $columns variable would be available to as $grid.columns.

```
// example/grids.scss
@mixin span(…) { … }
@function gutter(…) { … }
$columns: 12;

// my-file.scss
@use 'example/grids' as 'grid';

.column {
```

```
    @include grid.span(5 of $grid.columns);
    margin-bottom: grid.gutter();
}
```

Sass will default to using the filename as a prefix if none is provided, and also allow you to remove the prefix when you need to. It's still not clear if prefixing will work with placeholder selectors.

In addition to using a file with or without a given prefix, it might be possible to use an entire file *as a mixin*, so you can apply the code of that file anywhere you want—even in a nested context. The syntax is still under consideration, but it would make the entire CSS contents (that are not wrapped in a mixin) available to you as a single mixin.

Encapsulation

Modular imports will also give developers—especially library authors—more power over their public API. Currently, when you load a Sass library such as Susy, you gain access to pages and pages of undocumented functions that you'll never use. I've done my best to hide those functions behind long names like `_susy-valid-column-math`, but they still clutter the global namespace unnecessarily. With encapsulation, you'll have control over which mixins, functions, variables, and (possibly) placeholders should be made public. Adding - or _ to the start of a name will define it as private.

There is also talk of a `@forward` directive that would allow authors to pass the API from one module along as part of another. If you wanted to build a Susy flexbox extension, for example, you could tell your extension to forward the Susy API along to your users.

All of this, of course, is still in the works, and likely to change before it becomes available later in the year. I can't wait to see how it turns out—in what ways it changes Sass architecture, and helps the Sass ecosystem.

Wrapping Things Up

We've taken a fairly in-depth look at architecture for your Sass projects. We started off by discussing `@import`, and seeing how you can use it to split your project code into small logical units and organizing it across multiple files, partials and folders.

This forms the basis of any projects architecture. We then moved on to discuss a whole range of architecture options; which you choose will depend on your own projects and preferences. Finally we looked at future options for modular imports that should be in Sass 4.

Chapter **10**

The Sass Ecosystem

In my mind, the Sass ecosystem is where it all comes together. If you ask the Sass core developers, they'll tell you that the community is where it all starts. Sass first gained wide-spread attention when Chris Eppstein released Compass[1] in 2009, a project specifically designed to manage Sass packages and encourage open-source Sass code-sharing.

At that time, code-sharing in CSS meant copy-pasting libraries of prebuilt class names. Some people were sharing resets and grid systems, but that was about it. Eppstein saw an opportunity for Sass to change that, and help bring open-source collaboration to designers as CSS authors. And that, my friends, is the only reason I'm writing this book today.

But community wasn't the only drive behind Compass; it's also become a cornerstone philosophy in the Sass language design. As new features are added, Eppstein and his colleague Natalie Weizenbaum regularly discuss how these will affect the ability to share code and maintain consistency across Sass projects.

---

[1] http://compass-style.org

If you're just starting with Sass, or looking for suggestions on how to use it, there's a thriving community of newsletters, blogs, and podcasts to which you can turn. Sass News[2], created by Stuart Robson[3] and maintained by Jina Bolton[4], is a monthly email digest of Sass-related news. Sass Bites[5] by Micah Godbolt[6] is a podcast that offers Sass demonstrations, tutorials, and interviews every Thursday at noon (Pacific Time). The Sass Way[7] is a community blog offering Sass tutorials and articles for every level of experience. And, of course, many of the large web design sites (such as SitePoint[8] and CSS-Tricks[9]) provide regular Sass content as well. A quick web search will turn up many more.

Open-source Sass

When I first discovered Sass in 2009, there were only a few open-source Sass projects publicly available. Chris was working hard to change this, having just released Compass. To show what could be done, he included two grid systems with Compass—Sass ports of existing CSS grid systems: 960gs[10], and Blueprint[11]—with a few variables and mixins to make them customizable and semantic. Sass allowed you to use a grid without all those ugly classes! Yes, at one point that seemed special.

The Sass ecosystem has come a long way since then. Now you can find Sass libraries to help solve any number of common web design problems. Nearly 200 have been collected on Sache[12], a database of Sass extensions, and more are added regularly. You can even add your own, which we'd recommend! But that's the tip of the iceberg. The npm website shows almost 4,000 results for Sass, and GitHub returns over 14,000 results. It's hard to say what the actual numbers are, but if you want to solve a problem with Sass, you probably have several options from which to choose.

---

[2] http://www.sassnews.com/
[3] https://twitter.com/StuRobson
[4] https://twitter.com/jina
[5] https://www.youtube.com/user/sassbites
[6] https://twitter.com/micahgodbolt
[7] http://thesassway.com/
[8] http://www.sitepoint.com/html-css/css/sass-css/
[9] https://css-tricks.com/
[10] http://960.gs/
[11] http://www.blueprintcss.org/
[12] http://www.sache.in/

Whilst there are Sass libraries for everything, we can break them down into roughly four categories. There are the big **front-end frameworks** that provide all the common front-end patterns a site might need. The largest frameworks such as Bootstrap[13] and Foundation[14] take this to an extreme, providing Ikea-style website kits just waiting to be assembled. They're great if you're after a fast and simple solution, but as soon as you venture into unknown territory, you are on your own.

Many of the big frameworks are available in Sass, but a **Sass framework** generally looks a bit different. Rather than providing fully realized front-end patterns, the Sass frameworks provide all the Sass utilities and toolkits that you might need along the way: helpers for layout, accessibility, typography, and so on.

There are also **design component** libraries that focus on providing specific styles, such as glossy buttons or nice typography. These are often smaller and modular tools, but they can be even more opinionated than the big frameworks because they are trying to achieve a precise design outcome. They are useful if you have a look that you want to achieve, and are unsure how to get there—or you just want to get there quickly and consistently.

Finally, there are the abstract **toolkit** utilities that act more like a hammer: they're good at hitting things, but they don't care what's hit, or why. As a consultant, these are my favorite tools, because I can take them from one project to the next without any baggage or preconceptions. Most of the tools we've built fall into this category. Toolkits are useful if you want to make certain tasks easier while still building everything from scratch.

Those four categories aren't mutually exclusive, but they can be helpful for thinking about the code you depend on. One framework will often span all four categories, and any project might depend on a mix. For me, a good set of utilities and toolkits form the basis of every project—and usually follow me from one to the next. I use design components and frameworks rarely, only when a project specifically calls for it.

---

[13] http://getbootstrap.com/
[14] http://foundation.zurb.com/

Frameworks

Compass[15] was the first big Sass framework. It was primarily intended as a Sass package manager, but also included a library of common utilities for other Sass toolkits (Compass plugins) to reference. Compass provided a wide range of utilities, but became most popular for its vast library of CSS vendor-prefixing mixins. Rather than writing out all the prefixes for `animation` or learning each different `linear-gradient` syntax, you could simply use the appropriate Compass mixin or function.

Compass has reached the end of its life and is no longer being actively maintained, but ThoughtBot's **Bourbon**[16] provides a similar set of features. Both are Ruby gems:

```
gem install bourbon
gem install compass
```

And Bourbon is now also available as a Node package:

```
npm install bourbon
```

Both have been built around the official CSS3 syntax, so their APIs are often (but not always) identical. For example, both can take the following animation keyframes:

```
@include keyframes(grow) {
  from {
    @include transform(scale(0));
  }
  to {
    @include transform(scale(1));
  }
}
```

And return efficiently prefixed CSS for every browser:

```
@-webkit-keyframes grow {
  from {
    -webkit-transform: scale(0);
  }
```

---

[15] http://compass-style.org
[16] http://bourbon.io/

```
  to {
    -webkit-transform: scale(1);
  }
}

@keyframes grow {
  from {
    transform: scale(0);
  }
  to {
    transform: scale(1);
  }
}
```

Grids

Grid systems were quite popular when Sass first started to gain attention, and they are prime candidates for Sassification. Early CSS grids had little or no flexibility and involved bulky libraries of classes that were hard to read. Sass provided the tools for improvements.

As far as we know, **Susy**[17] was the first grid system for Sass. I originally designed it to achieve Natalie Downe's[18] math-heavy layout system. Her approach could not be represented in a CSS library, but was straightforward to replicate with Sass math. Whilst never setting out to be a grid-system author, the first thing I ever did with Sass was write the mixin that would later become Susy. Now a number of tools exist that all provide roughly the same features, with slight variations.

Susy is focused on flexibility, because you know what your project needs better than anyone else. While the quickest entry point for Susy is the span(..) mixin, its true power comes from the similarly named span(..) function and gutter(..) companion. The mixin provides float-based output, but the functions can be used anywhere to create any style of grid you can imagine; for example:

```
// Susy configuration:
$susy: (
  columns: 12, // the number of columns in a grid
```

---

[17] http://susy.oddbird.net/
[18] http://blog.natbat.net/post/46614243624/css-systems

```scss
  gutters: 1/4, // the size of a gutter relative to a column
);

// Span mixin:
article {
  @include span(8 of 12);
}

// Susy functions:
aside {
  flex: 1 1 span(4 of 12);
  margin-left: gutter();
}
```

```css
/* Compiled CSS */
article {
  width: 66.10169%;
  float: left;
  margin-right: 1.69492%;
}

aside {
  flex: 1 1 32.20339%;
  margin-left: 1.69492%;
}
```

Susy is available through Ruby gems, Bower, npm, and GitHub. Susy Three[19] is well underway at this point, with plans to simplify the configuration options and focus even more on the core functions—moving opinionated output into optional plugins.

Singularity[20] started with a strong focus on *asymmetrical* grids (columns not necessarily being all the same size), and has grown into a powerful and well-rounded grid toolkit. Created by Scott Kellum[21], and maintained by Sam Richard[22], Singularity explicitly manages the relationship between media queries and grids, asking you to define both up front.

---

[19] https://GitHub.com/oddbird/susy/tree/threeish

[20] https://github.com/at-import/Singularity/wiki

[21] https://twitter.com/ScottKellum

[22] https://twitter.com/Snugug

Singularity uses two primary values to define your grid: grids and gutters. At first, they seem similar to Susy's columns and gutters. Grids are defined with a unitless number of columns, or a list of unitless asymmetrical column sizes. Gutters are also defined with a unitless number, describing the ratio of a gutter to a single column. They are defined using the add-grid(..) and add-gutter(..) mixins:

```
// Symmetrical
@include add-grid(12);      // 12 columns
@include add-gutter(1/4);   // gutters are 1/4 the size of a column

// Asymmetrical
@include add-grid(1 3 5 7); // 4 uneven columns, sized relative to
➡each other
@include add-gutter(0.25)   // gutters are sized relative to
➡column-sizes
```

And that's where the similarities end. Singularity allows you to add new grids at explicit breakpoints:

```
@include add-grid(3);
@include add-grid(6 at 500px);
@include add-grid(1 3 5 7 at 900px);

@include add-gutter(1/3);
@include add-gutter(.25 at 900px);
```

Of course, Sass is unaware of the DOM, but if you use the Breakpoint plugin for media queries (see the next section), Singularity does know when it's being used inside a breakpoint that matches your description.

Media Queries

With the popularity of responsive design came a boom in the development of media query handling tools. Since media queries in CSS require a limited amount of repetition or prefixing, these tools mainly help to store and organize common breakpoints, providing syntax sugar along the way. They also have fallback options for (increasingly rare) browsers without support for media queries.

The first major media query plugin we knew about was Breakpoint[23], from Mason Wendell[24] and Sam Richard. Breakpoint starts by providing a sparse syntax for the most common min/max queries:

```
.mason::after {
  @include breakpoint(400px) {
    content: 'A single number is used as a min-width.';
  }

  @include breakpoint(400px 900px) {
    content: 'A pair of numbers are used for min- and max-width.';
  }

  @include breakpoint('height' 300px 500px) {
    content: 'You can also be explicit about the property, such as
➥ height.';
  }
}
```

```
@media (min-width: 400px) {
  .mason::after {
    content: 'A single number is used as a min-width.';
  }
}

@media (min-width: 400px) and (max-width: 900px) {
  .mason::after {
    content: 'A pair of numbers are used for min- and max-width.';
  }
}

@media (min-height: 300px) and (max-height: 500px) {
  .mason::after {
    content: 'You can also be explicit about the property, such as
➥ height.';
  }
}
```

The Breakpoint syntax expands from there to include every complex media query type you can imagine. It also furnishes several options for browser fallbacks in the

---

[23] https://github.com/at-import/breakpoint/wiki
[24] https://twitter.com/codingdesigner

original file, or separately. Perhaps most interesting (though I'd be pressed to name a use case), you can access details about the current media query at any time:

```
.sam::before {
  @include breakpoint(700px (orientation landscape)) {
    content: 'orientation: ' + breakpoint-get-context('orientation');
    content: 'min-width: ' + breakpoint-get-context('min-width');
    content: 'max-width: ' + breakpoint-get-context('max-width');
  }
}
```

```
@media (min-width: 700px) and (orientation: landscape) {
  .sam::before {
    content: "orientation: landscape";
    content: "min-width: 700px";
    content: "max-width: false";
  }
}
```

Eduardo Bouças[25] has his own take on media queries (with help from Hugo), called include-media[26]. Include-media starts with a map of predefined breakpoints, then uses >, <, =, and other comparison characters to turn them into full queries rendered by the media(..) mixin. Include-media also supplies built-in keywords for orientation, resolution, and media categories:

```
$breakpoints: (
  turtle: 320px,
  dog: 768px,
  giraffe: 1024px
);

.eduardo::before {
  @include media(">turtle", "<=dog") {
    content: 'Larger than turtle (320px), but smaller or equal to
```

---

[25] https://twitter.com/eduardoboucas
[26] http://include-media.com/

```
➥ dog (768px)';
  }
}
```

```
@media (min-width: 321px) and (max-width: 768px) {
  .eduardo::before {
    content: 'Larger than turtle (320px), but smaller or equal to
➥ dog (768px)';
  }
}
```

For my work, I rarely need anything as powerful as Breakpoint or include-media; it's mainly about keeping all my configurations in one place. I use a map like Eduardo's, with a set of "prepositional" mixins (above(..), below(..), and between(..)) to cover the common cases. Breakpoints can be set explicitly, but because I'm using Accoutrement-Layout[27] along with Accoutrement-Scale[28], I can instead reference layout sizes directly where they're defined:

```
// Layout Sizes
$sizes: (
  'page': 40em, // the max-width of my layout container
);

// Special Breakpoints
$breakpoints: (
  'toolbar-text': 15em, // a breakpoint for showing text beside
➥ toolbar icons
);

// Accoutrement Usage
.miriam {
  @include above('toolbar-text') {
    .toolbar-text { display: inline-block; }
  }

  @include below('page') {
```

---

[27] http://oddbird.net/accoutrement-layout/sassdoc/

[28] http://oddbird.net/accoutrement-scale/sassdoc/

```
    padding: 1em;
  }
}
```

Toolkits

The best Sass libraries are the utility toolkits that help you write better Sass without any opinion on the output styles you're creating. The popular Modular Scale[29] plugin from Scott Kellum helps you define "modular typographic scales" and access them across your project. Modular Scale configuration starts with two variables:

```
$ms-base: 1em;
$ms-ratio: $golden;
```

The `$ms-base` variable defines the starting point of the scale, while `$ms-ratio` defines the ratio between numbers. Modular Scale includes a long list of prenamed ratios, such as the default golden ratio, which represents a ratio of `1:1.618`. Starting with those defaults, the modular scale looks like this:

```
1em->1.61803em->2.61803em->4.23607em->6.8541em->11.09017em...
```

You can use the `ms(..)` function to access numbers up and down the scale, with a 0 index for the base number. Calling `ms(1)` will return `1.61803em`, `ms(2)` will return `2.61803em`, and so on. Modular Scale also allows you to start from multiple base numbers and intertwine multiple ratios for a more dense scale. There is also an `ms-respond(..)` mixin that will automatically adjust your font sizes across a range of the scale, from one predefined breakpoint to another.

Mathematical Constants Are Not Prefixed

Unlike other variables from Modular Scale, `$golden` is not prefixed with `$ms-` because it is a mathematical constant, and therefore does not need to namespaced.

---

[29] https://github.com/modularscale/modularscale-sass

Sassdash[30], an interesting utility by David Khourshid[31], is a Sass implementation of the popular lodash[32] JavaScript library. It's a high-level utility, designed to help toolkit authors write complex Sass more easily. If you're used to lodash, it should be known territory, as nearly the entire library has been ported. I'm unfamiliar with lodash, and this library is so vast it's hard to know where to start. Here's one clever function that plucks values from multiple maps based on a shared key:

```
$authors: (
  ('name': 'Hugo', 'origin': 'France'),
  ('name': 'Miriam', 'origin': 'Lesotho')
);

$origins: _pluck($authors, 'origin'); // ('France', 'Lesotho')
```

David also built Sassport[33], a toolkit for sharing JavaScript functions and values with your Sass. For example, you might define your color palette in JavaScript:

```
// my-colors.js
module.exports = {
  primary: '#C0FF33',
  secondary: '#BADA55'
};
```

And then access it in your Sass:

```
// stylesheet.scss
$colors: require('path/to/my-colors');
$primary: map-get($colors, 'primary');
```

Sassport is able to recognize different Sass data types (strings, maps, colors, and so on), and make the correct choice for translating data between JavaScript and Sass. You can also write JavaScript functions such as this one for the size of an image:

---

[30] https://github.com/davidkpiano/sassdash
[31] https://twitter.com/DavidKPiano
[32] https://lodash.com/
[33] https://github.com/davidkpiano/sassport

```
// index.js
var sassport = require('sassport');
var sizeOf = require('image-size');

sassport()
  .functions({
    'size-of($path)': sassport.wrap(function(path) {
      return sizeOf(path);
    }, { unit: 'px' })
  });
```

Now you can use that JavaScript function inside your Sass:

```
// stylesheet.scss
$image-size: size-of('miriam.png');

// resulting map:
$image-size: (
  'width': 145px,
  'height': 175px,
);
```

At OddBird, we use a set of modular but interconnected toolkits that we call Accoutrement[34]. The primary Accoutrement modules handle color and sizing palettes, providing a central configuration and functions for accessing those settings across a project.

Accoutrement-Color[35] starts with a map of colors to be used in the project. I like using maps to collect all my related values into one place, rather than having sixteen different variables. If we named sixteen color variables $color-pink, $color-red, and so on, we could see that they're related, but Sass doesn't know that. Putting them together in a map tells Sass that they're part of a single system, so we can loop through them in Sass. This is a feature I use regularly, especially when creating visual styleguides.

The downside is that map values are unable to easily reference other values in the same map. The following will fail to work because the $colors variable is yet to

---

[34] http://oddbird.net/accoutrement/
[35] http://oddbird.net/accoutrement-color/sassdoc/

actually exist at declaration time when we are trying to access it in the `tint(..)`
function:

```
// Maps can't reference themselves …
$colors: (
  'pink': hsl(330, 100%, 45%),
  'callout': tint(map-get($colors, 'pink'), 90%),
);
```

The accoutrement toolkits work around this by describing relationships in a consistent syntax and then resolving them at runtime. Here's the color map for my personal
website:

```
$colors: (
  // brand colors
  'light': #fff,
  'gray': hsl(0, 0%, 50%),
  'blue': hsl(195, 100%, 43%),
  'red': hsl(0, 100%, 50%),
  'pink': hsl(330, 100%, 45%),

  // site palette
  'primary': 'pink',
  'background': 'light',
  'text': 'gray' ('shade': 50%),

  'callout': 'primary' ('tint': 90%),
  'accent': 'blue' ('shade': 15%),

  'action': 'primary',
  'focus': 'accent',
  'overlay': 'background' ('rgba': 0.9),
  'shadow': 'text' ('rgba': 0.75),

  'title': 'action' ('shade': 15%),
  'border': 'title',
);
```

Then we use a `color(..)` function that is intelligent about accessing the map recurs-
ively (to follow each reference) and resolving the adjustments called for. Each ad-
justment includes the name of a color-adjustment function defined in Sass (e.g.
`rgba(..)`) or elsewhere in Accoutrement-Color (e.g. `tint(..)` and `shade(..)`), and

the necessary arguments to pass in addition to the color being adjusted. So `color('text')` will start by finding the value of `gray` (`hsl(0, 0%, 50%)`) and then calling `shade(hsl(0, 0%, 50%), 50%)` to return the result.

Accoutrement-Color also provides luminance and contrast tools based on the WCAG[36] guidelines for accessible color contrast. The `contrast(..)` function will return the best contrast from a list of options, while the `contrasted(..)` mixin outputs a background color with the best-contrasted text

```
// Sass input

.contrast {
  // get best contrast for 'pink' from either 'background' or 'text'
  color: contrast('pink', 'background', 'text');
}

.contrasted {
  @inlcude contrasted('pink', 'background', 'text');
}
```

```
/* CSS output */
.contrast {
  color: #fff;
}

.contrasted {
  background-color: hsl(330, 100%, 45%);
  color: #fff;
}
```

Accoutrement-Scale[37] works similarly, but describes common sizes to be used in a project: from font sizes and line-heights, to columns, gutters, border widths, and layout element widths. All of them can be defined explicitly or using a modular scale (based loosely on Scott Kellum's Modular Scale), and accessed in any comparable units. The `font-size(..)` function sets both font size and line heights based on the defined scale, and the `size(..)` function allows you to access any size on the fly.

---

[36] https://www.w3.org/WAI/intro/wcag
[37] http://oddbird.net/accoutrement-scale/sassdoc/

Accoutrement-Layout[38] provides media query tools that tie into existing scales, with additional tools for managing `z-index`, `box-sizing`, positioning, and other common layout issues. Accoutrement-Type[39] lets us define all our web fonts in one map and import them automatically with a single call to `@include import-webfonts`. Then font stacks can be applied with a call to `@include font-family('myFont')`. All the accoutrements play nicely together, so much so that we're working on a SassDoc-based living styleguide generator called Herman[40] to bring them all together (see later in the chapter for more on SassDoc).

Beautiful Code

Clean, beautiful code should be a goal in every project. If other developers need to make a change, they should be able to read what is there and understand it. Readable code is the core of maintainability, and the first step towards readable code is a good **linter**. Like a good spell-checker, the linter should catch all your small typos and formatting mistakes, so it's not left to others to do so. It's the first line of defense before a good code review with other developers.

There are several great linters for Sass: scss-lint[41] is a Ruby gem, and the newer sasslint[42] and stylelint[43], which are npm packages for Node. Both allow you to configure linting rules for your project, such as maximum nesting levels, leading zeros on decimals, and organization of properties in a block. You can even create your own rules as needed.

Sass Guidelines[44] are handy for organizing your project, setting up your linters, establishing naming conventions, and so on. Written by Hugo, it's an opinionated styleguide for your code; it might not all work for you, but it's a great place to start.

If you're using Sass variables, functions, and mixins, it's recommended that you document how they work. Toolkit authors will find it particularly important, but anyone who has extensive tooling built into their projects should also consider

---

[38] http://oddbird.net/accoutrement-layout/sassdoc/

[39] http://oddbird.net/accoutrement-type/sassdoc/

[40] https://github.com/oddbird/sassdoc-theme-herman

[41] https://github.com/brigade/scss-lint

[42] https://github.com/sasstools/sass-lint

[43] http://stylelint.io/

[44] http://sass-guidelin.es/

documentation for their team. Another great tool from Hugo is SassDoc[45], an npm package that parses your Sass comments and generates a beautiful static site with your documentation.

Here's the SassDoc comment for our `tint(..)` function in Accoutrement-Colors. It starts with a general description, and then explicitly documents each parameter and the expected return:

```
/// Mix a color with `white` to get a lighter tint.
///
/// @param {String | list} $color -
///    The name of a color in your palette,
///    with optional adjustments in the form of `(<function-name>:
➥ <args>)`.
/// @param {Percentage} $percentage -
///    The percentage of white to mix in.
///    Higher percentages will result in a lighter tint.
///
/// @return {Color} -
///    A calculated css-ready color-value based on your global color
➥ palette.
@function tint(
  $color,
  $percentage
) {
  /* … */
}
```

Using the default theme (from which there are several to choose, or you can design your own), SassDoc converts that comment into a static website, as shown in Figure 10.1.

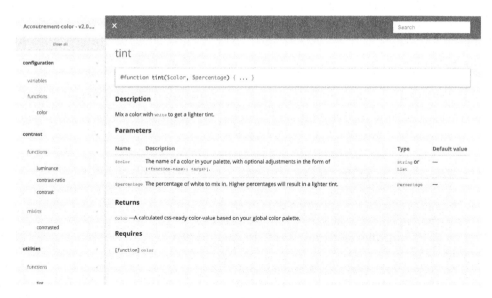

Figure 10.1. SassDoc Output

Testing is also important if you are doing anything complex with functions or mixins. It's a good way to ensure your code won't break any time you make adjustments, but it can also be helpful in developing new features. If you write the tests first, you'll know exactly if the feature works correctly when your tests pass!

True[46] is a unit-testing toolkit from yours truly, written in pure Sass so that it works anywhere Sass is compiled. The core testing happens in assertion functions: `assert-equal(..)`, `assert-unequal(..)`, `assert-true(..)`, and `assert-false(..)`. These are organized into tests, and can be grouped in test modules. Here's an example of True testing our `tint(..)` function:

```
@include test-module('Tint [function]') {
  @include test('Adjusts the tint of a color') {
    @include assert-equal(
      tint('primary', 25%),
      mix(#fff, color('primary'), 25%),
```

```
        'Returns a color mixed with white at a given weight.');
    }
}
```

When compiled, True will output CSS comments with detailed results, and warn you in the console if any tests fail:

```
/* # Module: Tint [function] */
/* ----------------------- */
/* Test: Adjusts the tint of a color */
/*    ✔ Returns a color mixed with white at a given weight. */

/* … */

/* # SUMMARY ---------- */
/* 16 Tests: */
/*   - 14 Passed */
/*   - 0 Failed */
/*   - 2 Output to CSS */
/* -------------------- */
```

What does it mean that two tests were "output to CSS" in this example? Those tests aren't shown, but they are testing mixin output. Using pure CSS, True can only confirm the results of function tests, so mixin tests are simply output to the CSS where they can be compared manually (gross) or with a CSS parser (better!). To make that easy, True integrates with JavaScript test runners such as Mocha[47], and has a Ruby command line interface written by Scott Davis[48]. Either one will parse the CSS output completely, including the output from mixins, and give you full results for both function and mixin tests:

```
Luminance [function]
   ✓ Returns luminance of a color

Contrast Ratio [function]
   ✓ Returns contrast ratio between two colors

Contrast [function]
   ✓ Dark on light
```

---

[47] https://mochajs.org/
[48] https://twitter.com/jetviper21

```
    ✓ Light on dark
    ✓ Default light fallback
    ✓ Default dark fallback
    ✓ Multiple contrast options

contrasted [mixin]
    ✓ Dark on light
    ✓ Light on dark

Tint [function]
    ✓ Adjusts the tint of a color

Shade [function]
    ✓ Adjusts the shade of a color

Color [function]
    ✓ Named color
    ✓ Referenced color
    ✓ Adjusted color
    ✓ Complex nesting of colors
    ✓ Multiple adjustment function arguments


16 passing (11ms)
```

Package Managers

There is no one way to share (or use) third-party Sass code, but there are several popular package managers that can be helpful. You can always copy and paste Sass into place, but that leaves you disconnected from the source. One of the advantages of using third-party code is that others help you update and maintain it. If you copy and paste third-party code, you're on your own. No one can send you bug fixes, patches, and updates.

You can also use a version control system such as git to download packages directly from an online repository like GitHub. That's a step in the right direction because now your copied code is linked back to its origin. You're part of a community!

Package managers take that one step further, allowing you to manage and update all your dependencies in one place. In the days before LibSass, most Sass libraries were distributed as Ruby Gems[49] and often managed through a tool such as Bundler[50]. Many Sass libraries are still available as gems, but it's becoming more common to see npm (and occasionally Bower) packages, since everyone has JavaScript in their stack already. Popular libraries are often available through all the major packaging systems.

If you're using RubyGems, Compass provides extra package management features specifically for Sass libraries. This allows those libraries to automatically register with the Sass compiler and provide static assets (JavaScript, images, and so on) in addition to Sass.

To package your library as a gem, you'll need a `gemspec` file in your project's root directory. A gemspec looks a little like this:

```
# miriam.gemspec
Gem::Specification.new do |s|
    s.name       = 'miriam'
    s.version    = '0.1.0'
    s.licenses   = ['MIT']
    s.summary    = "A Sassy toolkit named after me."
    s.authors    = ["Miriam Suzanne"]
    s.email      = 'miriam@oddbird.net'
    s.files      = Dir.glob("lib/*.*")
    s.files     += Dir.glob("sass/**/*.*")
    s.homepage   = 'http://oddbird.net/'
end
```

Making your gem self-register with Sass requires a Ruby lib file as well. Here's some code I copy from one project to another, changing the names as necessary. It starts by registering with Compass if it's available, otherwise it uses an environment variable. Not sure what that all means? Don't worry—I do it without knowing any Ruby, and just reading directions and copy-pasting code from other Sass libraries:

```
# lib/miriam.rb
miriam_stylesheets_path = File.expand_path(File.join(File.dirname
➡(__FILE__), '..', 'sass'))
ENV['SASS_PATH'] ||= ''
```

---

[49] https://rubygems.org
[50] http://bundler.io/

```
begin
  require 'compass'
  ENV['SASS_PATH'] = ENV['SASS_PATH'] + File::PATH_SEPARATOR +
➥ Compass.configuration.sass_load_paths.join(File::PATH_SEPARATOR)
rescue LoadError
end

# Compass not found, register on the Sass path via the environment.
ENV['SASS_PATH'] += File::PATH_SEPARATOR + miriam_stylesheets_path
```

If you're packaging for Compass, you can also add a short Compass lib file:

```
# lib/compass-miriam.rb
require 'miriam'
```

With `miriam.gemspec` and your lib files in place, you can run `gem build miri-am.gemspec` to build the package, and `gem push miriam-0.1.0.gem` to make it available online. Using a release naming pattern such as SemVer[51] will help your users understand what's contained in each release.

Packaging with npm or Bower is simpler, in my opinion. Bower is an npm package itself, so either way you'll start by installing Node[52] and npm. With that in place, both require slight variations on a JSON file (**package.json** or **bower.json**), which will be created for you if you run `npm init` or `bower init` and answer the required questions. If you register on the respective sites, you can then `bower register` (a one-time command) or `npm publish` (every time you release a new version). Bower doesn't require version updates because it relies on GitHub tags instead.

Bower users can install your package with something along the lines of `bower install miriam`, and npm users can `npm install miriam`. Your package will be downloaded into their `bower_components/` or `node_modules/` folders, respectively.

Eyeglass[53] is a more trimmed down Sass package manager that Chris Eppstein (the creator of Compass) has been working on. It uses npm in place of Ruby Gems, since the community is moving in that direction with LibSass. To mark your library as

---

[51] http://semver.org/

[52] https://nodejs.org/en/

[53] https://github.com/sass-eyeglass/eyeglass

an Eyeglass module, add `eyeglass-module` as a keyword in your npm **package.json** file, along with a brief `eyeglass` block:

```
{
  …
  "keywords": ["eyeglass-module", "sass", …],
  "eyeglass": {
    "name": "miriam", # the name of your module
    "needs": "^0.6.0" # the version of eyeglass required
  },
  …
}
```

Eyeglass also allows you to extend Sass with JavaScript functions and pass along static assets. The tool is still pre-1.0, but there are a number of interesting features on the way, so it's worth keeping an eye on.

There's no right answer for code-sharing and package managers, but as community is the goal, try to go along with the crowd on these decisions. Look around to see what your community is doing, and follow suit.

A Sassy Wrap!

This is a lot of information to digest—so we recommend forgetting all of it. Go grab a cookie, make yourself some tea, and start playing around with live code on Sass-meister[54] or CodePen[55]. The Web is a young field, and Sass an even younger language—there is plenty to explore!

You don't have to design Twittstrap and have a million followers to be an active part of the community. Start by playing around, looking for better solutions to the problems you face every day. For me, Sass toolkits are the byproduct of my work. Whenever I notice my code becoming repetitive or difficult to maintain, I look for the patterns. Often, my first solution to a problem is over-engineered, over-opinionated, and over-specific—but after using it for a while, I'm able to trim it down to the essence.

---

[54] http://www.sassmeister.com/
[55] http://codepen.io/

Start by solving your own problems using other people's solutions as a reference point. Then share your solutions, and receive feedback. This book's authors (Hugo[56] and Miriam[57]) are both on Twitter, as are the core Sass designers (Natalie Weizenbaum[58] and Chris Eppstein[59]) and the rest of the community. Talk to us! Share your toys! We're excited to see what you build.

---

[56] https://twitter.com/hugogiraudel
[57] https://twitter.com/mirisuzanne
[58] https://twitter.com/nex3
[59] https://twitter.com/chriseppstein

CPSIA information can be obtained at www.ICGtesting.com
Printed in the USA
BVOW09s1437120616

451732BV00011B/44/P